## RACEHORSE IN THE RAIN

The horses were now less than a hundred yards away. Mandy could hear the rasping sound of their breathing and felt the thundering of their hooves on the turf. Bright Spark was still in front, looking every bit a champion as he galloped toward the last hurdle.

"Go, Bright Spark!" yelled James.

Mandy laughed. "No harm in us practicing for the big race, too, I guess!"

But when Bright Spark was barely a yard away from the jump, Mandy heard Mark draw his breath in sharply. "Wrong stride! He's too close," he muttered.

Bright Spark's head shot up as he reached the hurdle. He pawed with his front legs, but there was no room to take off. . . .

*Give someone you love a home!*
*Read about the animals of Animal Ark™*

# RACEHORSE in the RAIN

Ben M. Baglio

Illustrations by Ann Baum

Cover illustration by
Mary Ann Lasher

AN
**APPLE**
PAPERBACK

SCHOLASTIC INC.

New York  Toronto  London  Auckland  Sydney
Mexico City  New Delhi  Hong Kong  Buenos Aires

# Special thanks to Andrea Abbot

ISBN 0-439-68496-X

12 11 10 9 8 7 6 5 4 3 2                    4 5 6 7 8 9/0

Printed in the U.S.A.                    40
First Scholastic printing, November 2004

# *One*

"Hello, Grandpa! You'd like to buy another raffle ticket, wouldn't you?" Mandy Hope greeted her grandpa as he pushed open the door of Lilac Cottage. "Gran's taken two more," she added persuasively.

Tom Hope kicked off his rubber boots and came into the kitchen. "No, thanks, dear. I think I've bought enough." He smiled at Mandy, who was perched on a stool at the kitchen table helping her best friend, James Hunter, to unravel a tangled string of tiny silver lights.

Mandy's gran was measuring some flour. She put

1

down the plastic container and looked across at Grandpa Hope, her hands on her hips. "You old miser, Tom!" she said, and frowned.

Grandpa slid his feet into a pair of well-worn slippers. "Miser!" he echoed with mock outrage. "When I've already bought six tickets?" He shook his head indignantly.

Mandy wasn't put off by her grandpa's protests. She and James still had twelve tickets left to sell, and Mandy was determined to sell every last one. All the money raised was going to Betty Hilder's animal sanctuary on the edge of the village. Mandy's parents often helped Betty with the strays and injured wildlife she took in. Adam and Emily Hope were both vets who ran Animal Ark, the veterinary practice that was attached to their home in the Yorkshire village of Welford.

Mandy wrinkled her nose at her grandfather. "You've only bought six?" she teased. She looked at James across the table. "How many tickets did you say *your* grandpa bought, James?"

"Er, seven," grinned James. "Isn't that right Blackie?" he added. He reached down to pat his dog, a glossy black Labrador who was sitting beside his chair. Blackie gave a short bark.

"That's emotional blackmail," said Tom Hope, laughing. "I won't fall for it."

Gran winked at Mandy and James. "We'll just have to use another tactic to get him to part with his money." She chuckled as she pulled on a pair of oven mitts, then opened the oven door. A delicious aroma filled the kitchen.

"Mmm! Smells good," said Grandpa Hope as Gran took out a big tray of mince pies, then put them on a wire rack on the table to cool.

With only two weeks to go before Christmas, Gran was very busy producing her famous mince pies to sell at the Christmas fair.

"One of those would go down well with a cup of tea," Grandpa said hopefully. He poured boiling water into a teapot and carried it over to the table where Mandy was setting out cups and saucers. As he put the pot down, Grandpa knocked the edge of the cooling rack, and a piece of crust broke off one of the pies.

He reached over to pick it up but Gran tapped his hand. "No, you don't!" she said.

"It's just a crumb!" protested Grandpa.

"No ticket, no pie," Gran said firmly.

"Now that's plain bribery," said Tom Hope, folding his arms. "You can't do that, Dorothy."

"Oh, no? Just watch me," replied Gran. "Help your-selves, Mandy and James," she added, nodding at the rack of steaming pies.

"Yum!" said James, putting down the string of lights and quickly selecting a tart.

Mandy looked pointedly at her grandpa, picked up the broken crust he'd been eyeing, and popped it into her mouth. "Mmm. Delicious!" she declared.

"Oh, all right, you win," said Grandpa Hope. He reached into his pocket and took out some coins. "Here, Mandy. I'd have bought another one anyway." He smiled. "And who knows, this one could be the winning ticket. What did you say the main prize was?"

"I didn't," she told him, taking a sheet of paper out of her pocket and giving it to her grandpa, who wrote his name next to one of the numbers. "It's a mystery prize. Only Mrs. McFarlane knows what it is."

"Maybe the winner will get a year's supply of free stamps," suggested James.

Mandy laughed. "Great for mailing Christmas cards! But I don't think that's what it'll be. Perhaps it'll be something to do with animals, since the raffle's to help the animal sanctuary."

"Like a free vet check at Animal Ark?" James guessed.

"Actually, Mom and Dad did donate a free checkup as one of the prizes," Mandy revealed. "But that's definitely not the main one." She put the coins in a can and did a quick count in her head. "We've sold ninety tickets so far."

Gran looked impressed. "Well done!"

Mandy frowned. "It's OK. But we really want to sell all of them, for Betty's sake. The trouble is, we've run out of buyers. Just about everyone in Welford has taken at least one ticket." She put the lid on the can and dropped it into her backpack.

James took a bite of his mince pie and had to suck in his breath because the filling was still piping hot. When he managed to swallow, he said, "We're also running out of time, since the drawing's in a few hours."

The Grand Drawing was to take place that evening during a family Christmas party at the Fox and Goose, the local restaurant that was run by Julian and Sara Hardy.

"Maybe you should try more bribery," said Grandpa. "It worked on me." He gave Gran a sideways look.

"I don't like to think of it as bribery," Gran responded. "More like gentle persuasion."

Mandy folded up the raffle sheet and put it back in her pocket. "OK, then. This is what we'll do. We'll march everyone from the village to Lilac Cottage. Then Gran can dangle mince pies in front of them to persuade them to buy our tickets," she joked.

Gran poured herself another cup of tea. "That's not a bad idea," she said thoughtfully.

"I'm just teasing," Mandy said. "I'm not really going to bring the whole village here."

"I know, dear," Gran replied, taking a sip of tea. "But I think my mince pies *could* help you out. Why don't you offer a free pie with every ticket sold?"

"Are you sure you don't mind?" Mandy said.

"Of course not. I'm only too happy to help out," said Gran warmly. "And I can easily make some more."

"Then it's a great idea!" Mandy exclaimed. She jumped up and flung her arms around her grandmother. The tea in Gran's cup sloshed, threatening to spill onto the table.

"Careful." Mandy's grandmother chuckled as she held the cup steady.

Meanwhile, Grandpa was jangling some coins in his pocket. "Now that's what I call a decent offer. I think I'll take another ticket," he decided.

Mandy laughed. "Good for you, Grandpa! Come on, James, let's go find some more customers."

"What are we going to do? Knock on people's doors?" asked James, clipping the leash onto Blackie's collar.

"We could do that," Mandy agreed. "And if that doesn't work we can go to the post office. There are always lots of people there on Saturday morning." She climbed onto a stool and reached for a wicker basket on top of a cupboard. "Do you mind if we use this?" she asked Grandma Hope, jumping down with it. "I can sling it over my handlebars."

"Good idea," said Gran. She carefully wrapped eleven mince pies in a clean cloth, then put them in the basket along with a stack of paper napkins.

Grandpa pushed back his chair and stood up to gather the teacups. A smattering of crumbs fell off his lap and onto the floor. Blackie shot forward, pulling the leash out of James's hand, and licked up the crumbs.

"You're just like a vacuum cleaner," James said to his dog. "I bet you'd sniff out the smallest atom if you thought you could eat it."

"That's a Labrador for you." Grandpa laughed, carrying the cups to the sink.

"Perhaps you ought to leave Blackie here while you're out selling those tickets," Gran suggested. "In case he decides to help you get rid of the mince pies when you're not looking!"

"Thanks," said James. "I can't exactly trust him when there's food around."

Leaving Blackie happily gnawing on a bone that Gran had in her fridge, Mandy and James pedaled off toward the village.

"There's a potential customer," said James, looking ahead.

Not far from the Lilac Cottage was Rose Cottage, where Mrs. Jackson, a widow, lived. Mandy could see her working in the garden in the soft winter sunshine. "Morning, Mrs. Jackson," she called out, skidding to a stop next to the hedge.

Mrs. Jackson looked up from the rose bed she was working on. "Good morning, you two. Ready for the party tonight?"

"You bet!" said James. "But first we have to sell all our raffle tickets."

"You shouldn't have any trouble. There are some wonderful prizes. And it's for such a good cause," said Mrs. Jackson. "I've taken a couple of tickets myself."

"Well, if you buy another one, you'll win a sort of predrawing prize," ventured James.

Mrs. Jackson frowned. "A predrawing prize?"

"Yes. One of these," said Mandy. "They're fresh from the oven." She slipped the basket off her handlebars and unwrapped the cloth inside. Dusted with powdered sugar, the mince pies looked irresistible.

"Those can only be Dorothy's," said Mrs. Jackson appreciatively. "No one in Welford can touch her when it comes to baking. I'll definitely take another ticket." She rummaged about in the pocket of her slacks and pulled out some coins. Mandy wrote her name on the sheet and handed her one of the mince pies wrapped in a paper napkin.

"That was easy," remarked James as they pedaled on.

They parked their bikes outside the post office in the center of the village and before long had their next customers, Reverend Hadcroft and Bill Ward, the postman.

"I'll take two, please," said Reverend Hadcroft.

"And I'll have three," Bill Ward said. "One each for me and Jane." Jane was his wife. "And one extra to help me keep my strength up while I'm delivering the mail," he added, hoisting his heavy bag onto his shoulder.

Next to be tempted were Joan and Marjorie Spry, elderly twin sisters who were on their way to mail their Christmas cards. They bought two each, then bustled off, the pies safely stowed in the huge shopping basket that they carried between them.

"Can you believe it?" James exclaimed to Mandy. "From eleven tickets, we're down to the last one."

"It's even easier than I thought it would be." Mandy smiled.

"Let's go to Animal Ark to see if we can persuade Jean or Simon to buy it," suggested James.

Jean Knox was the receptionist at Animal Ark, and Simon was the nurse. But the first person Mandy and James met when they walked into the reception room was Mandy's dad.

"Would you like one of Gran's mince pies?" Mandy asked him casually.

"Would I like one? What a question," said Dr. Adam, holding out his hand and laughing.

"Actually it's a trick question," James admitted, and he put the raffle sheet into Dr. Adam's hand.

"What's this?" Mandy's dad frowned. "I've already bought ten tickets, remember?"

Mandy explained about the free mince pie.

"Trust you and your gran to be in cahoots." But Dr. Adam went over to the reception desk and opened the petty cash tin.

Just then, Jean came in from one of the examining rooms carrying a patient's file. "What are you doing with the petty cash?" she said sternly, looking at Dr. Adam over the top of her glasses.

"Er, nothing. Just making a donation to a very good cause," said Dr. Adam innocently. He handed the money to Mandy. "Don't worry, I'll put the money back when the clinic hours are over," he added.

"It's got to be a lucky ticket," James told him, "since it's our last one."

Dr. Adam examined the raffle sheet. "Z20. With a number like that, I'll be lucky if I win the booby prize," he said, and laughed.

Almost everyone from Welford was at the Christmas party at the Fox and Goose that night. Julian and Sara Hardy had strung up hundreds of tiny silver lights along the eaves, while inside, red and green decorations gave the restaurant a festive air. Mandy and James sat at a huge round table with their parents, Gran and Grandpa Hope, Mrs. McFarlane, and Betty Hilder.

After everyone had enjoyed the delicious buffet, Sara Hardy stood up and tapped a glass with a spoon. "Time for the Grand Drawing," she announced. "As our champion ticket sellers, Mandy and James are going to draw the winning tickets," she added with a smile.

Mandy and James grinned at each other as everyone clapped. Then they stood up and went over to join Sara. James pulled the first winning number out of a metal tankard that Sara was holding. "G15," he read aloud.

Mandy flicked through the raffle sheets until she came to the one marked G. She read out the name next to the number fifteen. "Rachel Farmer."

"Hooray!" came a voice from the back of the room, and ten-year-old Rachel pushed her way to the front, a wide smile on her face. "What have I won?" she asked.

Sara gave Rachel an envelope. "A year's subscription to a wildlife magazine," she declared.

Rachel looked delighted as she tore open the envelope. "Wow! Twelve copies of *Wild Ways.*"

"A perfect prize for you." Mandy smiled. She knew how much Rachel adored the animals and that, like Mandy, she wanted to be a vet one day.

James pulled out the next winning ticket. This time it belonged to Mrs. Ponsonby.

"What is it?" someone called out as the large, brightly dressed woman opened her prize envelope and took out a piece of paper. Standing next to her, Mandy could see the Animal Ark crest stamped at the top of the paper.

"A free vet check at Animal Ark," Mrs. Ponsonby read out in her booming voice. "What a splendid idea!"

Mandy tried hard not to laugh. Mrs. Ponsonby had two dogs, a Pekingese named Pandora and Toby, a mongrel. They were probably the most pampered dogs in Welford. The dogs had only to sneeze or not finish their food and Mrs. Ponsonby would be on the phone to Animal Ark.

"I bet it won't be long before she uses her prize," James whispered to Mandy.

Sara read out the winning numbers for the next ten prizes. Mandy was delighted when Mrs. Jackson won a basket of cheese and crackers, and Reverend Hadcroft drew an enormous box of cookies donated by a bakery in the nearby town of Walton. "You'd all better stop by the vicarage for tea to help me get through these," he told Mandy as he carried the cookies back to his table.

Finally, it was time for the Grand Mystery Prize. There was total silence while James closed his eyes dramatically and dipped into the container for the last time. He took out the piece of paper and called out the number. "Z20."

"Z20?" Mandy gasped. "That's Dad's ticket!"

"So it *was* the lucky ticket." Dr. Adam smiled as he came forward.

Mandy couldn't wait to find out what her dad had won.

"Well, how about that!" exclaimed Dr. Adam, tearing open the golden envelope. He handed Mandy the card. The words HARE HILL TRAINING YARD were painted along the top in black writing, and the card had a beautiful picture of a horse in one corner.

Mandy quickly read the wording on the card, feeling excitement bubble inside her like soda pop. "I don't believe it, Dad!" she burst out. "You've won a racehorse for the day!"

# *Two*

Early the next morning, the Hopes picked up James, then drove to Hare Hill to meet Bright Spark, Dr. Adam's prize racehorse. Mandy's dad had spoken to the owner of the yard, Mark Sheldon, after the party and accepted an invitation to meet the thoroughbred before the big day.

"Mr. Sheldon said that Bright Spark's the newest horse at Hare Hill," Mandy told James as they drove across the moor. "And he'll be racing at Lingwood Park the day after Christmas."

"Which is the day I get to own him," said Dr. Adam, turning off the road and onto the gravel driveway lead-

14

ing to Hare Hill. Soon the drive forked, and a sign indicated that the stable yard was to the right.

They drove past lush green pastures with neat post-and-rail fencing before pulling up outside a block of red-brick stables where Mark Sheldon was waiting for them. "We'll go right to Bright Spark's stall," the blond, friendly faced man told them. "Then I'll drive you up to the course so you can watch him and the others training."

"Great!" said Mandy. She could hardly wait to set eyes on the racehorse. Even so, she and James paused at each stall to pet the horses who were peering out inquisitively over the stall door. The horses seemed to be in perfect condition, with coats as sleek as velvet and bright, clear eyes. "They're so beautiful." Mandy sighed happily.

"Are they all yours?" James asked Mark as they approached the end of the block. He glanced back at the seven stalls they'd passed so far.

Mark shook his head. "No. Only three are, including Bright Spark. I train the others for their owners. Here we are," he announced, stopping outside the last stall. "This is Bright Spark."

Hearing his owner's voice, the racehorse pushed his head over the stall door and whinnied eagerly. He was a glossy bright bay with a jet-black mane and a white blaze running down his face.

"He's awesome!" Mandy whispered.

Bright Spark held her gaze for a moment, then snorted.

Mandy reached up and smoothed his face. "You'll be racing for Animal Ark the day after Christmas," she told him. "And this is your temporary owner." She stepped aside to let her dad pat the magnificent racehorse.

"Aren't you a splendid fellow?" murmured Dr. Adam, rubbing Bright Spark's neck.

Mark beamed. "I'm glad you like him. We have high

hopes that he'll develop into a top steeplechaser. Who knows, one day we could see him in the Grand National!"

A tall, dark-haired young man wearing jodhpurs and carrying a bridle and saddle crossed the yard to join them. "Morning, all," he said before opening the stall door and going inside.

"Hi, Phil. This is Phil Grimley," Mark explained to the Hopes and James. "He's Bright Spark's boy, which is another name for a groom. He's a future jockey, too, we hope."

"He looks too tall to be a jockey," James whispered to Mandy.

Mark overheard him. "Phil's certainly too tall to be a flat-race jockey," he agreed. "But he wants to be a steeplechase jockey, which involves racing over jumps, so his height doesn't matter. Steeplechase jockeys can be a bit heavier than flat-race jockeys."

"I suppose what's more important is that they're good at judging distances and fences," suggested Mandy's mom.

"That's right," Mark nodded. "Phil's been with us only a short time, but I'm already impressed with his riding skills."

"Will he be riding Bright Spark on December 26?" Mandy asked.

"No. Hare Hill's lead jockey, Gary Hart, will be in the saddle. Phil's not quite ready for the big races yet," said Mark. "But you'll see him riding Bright Spark today because Gary's working with another horse."

Inside the stall, Phil was tacking up Bright Spark. The horse turned his exquisite head to blow softly on Phil's neck as he checked that the girth was tight enough. "Come on, boy," Phil said, smiling, as he led the horse outside.

Out in the open, Bright Spark looked even more beautiful. His legs shone like ebony and his coat gleamed in the pale December sun. Phil walked him in a circle, and Mandy saw the horse's muscles rippling on his shoulders. There wasn't an animal on the planet that Mandy didn't love, but she had to admit that Bright Spark was the most stunning horse she'd ever seen.

"He looks like a winner to me," she declared. "I bet he'll do really well in the big race."

Phil shrugged. "Yeah, well, we'll see," he muttered.

Mandy felt puzzled. In the stable, it had been obvious that Phil loved Bright Spark. "That's odd," she said quietly to James. "You'd think he'd be really excited about Bright Spark running in such a big race."

James frowned. "Maybe he's nervous for him."

Mandy nodded. "Could be."

"Ready, Phil?" Mark called.

Phil nodded, then led Bright Spark over to the mounting block and swung himself into the saddle.

Meanwhile, more horses were being led out of their stalls. Mandy counted eleven, but none of them was as handsome as Bright Spark.

A long-legged chestnut gelding from two stalls down stamped his hooves restlessly, then reared up on his hind legs when his groom brought the reins over his head.

Mandy took a few steps back and felt her dad put a protective arm around her shoulder, while next to her, her mom sucked in her breath.

"That one's high-strung," observed James, sounding wary.

"That's Jackdaw's Lad. He belongs to my mother," said Mark. "He's quite a handful but a superb sprinter."

A jockey strode over to Jackdaw's Lad. He was short and wiry, fitting the picture that Mandy had always had of jockeys, and looked tiny next to the big, powerful horse. He took the reins from the groom and calmed the horse with a few quiet words.

"He's got a good touch," Mandy remarked admiringly.

"That's Gary Hart," Mark told her. "He's very experienced and a great jockey."

The rest of the jockeys came over and mounted their horses, then clattered out of the yard with Phil and

Bright Spark in front. The bay thoroughbred looked relaxed and confident as he turned onto the well-worn path that led up to the course on the moor above the stable yard.

"There's a good omen," said Dr. Adam. "My horse leading the field."

"And that's what we expect him to do at Lingwood Park," said Mark, walking toward his Range Rover, which was parked on the gravel drive. "It's quite a steep haul to the course, so we'll go by car. Hop in."

Mandy could hardly wait to see the horses in action. She climbed into the back of the Range Rover and squashed up next to her dad and James while her mom sat in the front next to Mark. They were about to drive away when frantic yapping broke out from inside one of the stalls.

"What's that?" Mandy asked, winding down her window.

Mark pulled up the hand brake. "Oops! I nearly forgot Parsley." He flung open his door and jumped out.

At the same time, Mandy saw a short-haired tan-and-white Jack Russell terrier scramble over the stall door, then come tearing across the yard to the Range Rover. "Look!" she exclaimed.

Mark crouched down, and the little dog leaped into his arms. "Sorry, Parsley." He laughed as the terrier licked him all over his face, her long thin tail whipping against his chest. He climbed back into the driver's seat and handed the dog to Mandy's mom. "This enthusiastic little one is Jackdaw's Lad's best friend," Mark explained, releasing the brake. "Ever since she was a puppy, she has insisted on going everywhere with that horse. I owned Parsley's mom, Florence, and Parsley was actually born in Jack's stall, so I guess it's not surprising."

"Does she even go to races?" Mandy asked, leaning forward and scratching the terrier's head.

Parsley responded by scrambling between the front seats and sitting on Mandy's lap. Mandy put an arm around the little dog and chuckled.

"Well, she always insists on coming in the horse van," said Mark in answer to Mandy's question. "But we have to be very careful about letting her out, because not many thoroughbreds like having a Jack Russell terrier under their feet."

Dr. Adam nodded. "I imagine that's right," he said.

Mark steered the Range Rover along a narrow lane that wound its way up the steep hill. In the distance, Mandy could see the racehorses making their way across the rugged moor, the jockeys hunched against the biting December wind. On her lap, Parsley stood on her hind legs, her front paws resting on the windowsill as she stared out excitedly.

"Not far now," said Mark, changing to a lower gear as the road grew steeper.

"I bet the horses must get plenty of exercise just going up to the course," remarked James.

Mandy glanced back the way they'd come. The red-brick stable nestled below them in a green valley surrounded by vast stretches of empty moorland. The Animal Ark Land Rover looked like a toy car from up here. On her lap, she felt Parsley begin to tremble with excitement. Did this mean they were about to arrive at the track? Mandy looked ahead, craning her neck as Mark drove into a field on top of the moor. Apart from a grove of trees at the top of a gentle slope, it was bordered by nothing but sky.

"Wow!" Mandy heard James exclaim. "It's like being on top of the world."

"It certainly is spectacular," agreed Dr. Emily.

A wide turf track ran along one side of the field, sloping upward for about a third of the distance before leveling out to form a straight track that ran parallel with the grove of trees. The tall, leafless trees swayed and rustled in the icy wind that swept across the moor. There was a series of hurdles on this stretch of track, flexible wooden fences about a yard high.

Mark parked the Range Rover next to the railings near the end of the track. Holding Parsley in her arms,

Mandy pushed open her door and jumped down onto the springy grass of the turf. She gazed along the runs and saw that six of the horses were circling at the bottom of the hill. She could just make out a white blaze on one of them. "I think I can see Bright Spark," she said to James as he climbed out behind her. "I wish I'd brought my binoculars," she added, tucking Parsley under one arm and climbing onto the railings to get a better look.

"Here, use these," said Mark, giving her a pair. "I always carry some spares in the Range Rover."

There was a pair for James, too, and he sat next to Mandy on the top rail and focused the powerful field glasses on the horses.

A heavy black cloud rolled across the sky, blocking out the sun for a few seconds. At the same time, the wind picked up, making Mandy shiver. She wasn't the only one. Parsley was shaking from the cold, too. "Here. Snuggle up close," she said, tucking the little dog inside her jacket and pulling up the zipper until only a brown-and-white nose peeped out. "That's better, isn't it?" She smiled at the bright little face looking up at her.

Mandy's mom pulled up the hood of her jacket. "Looks like we're in for some rain."

"Let's hope it holds off for awhile," said Dr. Adam.

"It should," said Mark, glancing up at the sky before training his binoculars on the group of horses and jockeys. He raised a hand, and Mandy saw one of the jockeys signal back to him before crouching forward and shortening his horse's reins.

"And they're off," said James, imitating a race commentator as the horses bunched together for a moment, then sprang forward to gallop up the track.

Mandy lifted her binoculars. She could see Jackdaw's Lad in the middle of the field and Bright Spark on the far side. Between them were a dapple gray and a dark chestnut, their jockeys crouched low over their horses' necks. "They're pretty level with each other," she observed. "Does that mean they can all run at the same speed?"

"I don't think they're actually racing at this point," pointed out her mom, leaning forward on the railing.

"You're right," said Mark, not taking his eyes off the horses. "They're working at half speed, which is quite a lot slower than a racing gallop. But once they reach the top of the hill, they'll pick up the pace."

Sure enough, the horses accelerated as they crested the hill and approached the first of the hurdles. Mandy concentrated on Bright Spark, who seemed to float over the ground, his long legs pounding tirelessly beneath him. Phil sat very still as the horse lengthened his stride, pulling away from the other horses as they reached the first hurdle.

Mandy's pulse quickened as she watched Bright Spark soar over the fence, not even clipping the brush with a hoof, then gallop on smoothly to the next hurdle. "He *is* good," she whispered, seeing Bright Spark open up even more of a lead.

Dr. Adam watched his prize horse appreciatively. "My money's definitely on him for the big race," he said, grinning.

The horses were now less than a hundred yards away. Mandy could hear the rasping sound of their breathing and felt the thundering of their hooves on the turf. Magnified by the binoculars, they became a wall of muscle, flashing eyes, and pounding legs. Feeling her stomach churn with excitement, she lowered the binoculars. Bright Spark was still in front, looking every bit a champion as he galloped toward the last hurdle.

"Go, Bright Spark!" yelled James.

Mandy laughed. "No harm in us practicing for the big race, too, I guess!" She watched Phil shorten the reins and close his legs against Bright Spark's flanks and waited breathlessly to see the horse clear the final hurdle.

But when Bright Spark was barely a yard away from the jump, Mandy heard Mark draw his breath in sharply. "Wrong stride! He's too close," he muttered.

Bright Spark's head shot up as he reached the hurdle. He pawed with his front legs, but there was no room to take off, and he crashed through the fence, unseating Phil, who was catapulted through the air.

"Oh, no!" Mandy cried out in horror as she saw Bright Spark stumble, his legs buckling. With a heart-stopping thud, the horse collapsed onto the ground and landed heavily on his side. The other horses swerved to avoid him as they landed, their jockeys snatching at the reins to keep control. Mandy's hand shot up to her mouth, stifling another cry. Desperately, she looked across at Phil, expecting to see him get up and run back to Bright Spark, who was heaving himself up.

But Phil didn't move. He lay still in a crumpled heap on the far side of the track, his head bent back and his limbs folded awkwardly beneath him.

# *Three*

Mandy felt the blood drain from her face. *Get up, Phil*, she urged silently.

"Watch out!" James yelled, and Mandy looked back at Bright Spark in time to see him scramble to his feet and gallop straight toward them.

Mandy felt a moment's relief that Bright Spark's legs were OK, but at the same time her own seemed to turn to stone. With the racehorse hurtling toward her, she couldn't move. Her dad grabbed her arm in the nick of time. "Out of the way!" he shouted, pulling her clear of the bolting horse.

With flared nostrils and the whites of his eyes flashing, Bright Spark galloped wildly past the Range Rover. A bristling hedge, thick with hawthorn and glossy-leafed rhododendrons, lay between the horse and the grove of trees.

"He's going to crash into the hedge," Mandy cried. She willed Bright Spark to slow down, but he met the hedge at full tilt.

"He'll never make it!" James exclaimed as the race-horse lifted off the ground, his front legs tucked under his chest and his back legs stretching out behind him.

But Bright Spark proved James wrong. With the stirrups flapping at his sides, the horse soared over the hedge. He landed with a thud on the other side, almost losing his footing in the tangled undergrowth, then cantered to the trees.

"Someone's got to go after him!" Mandy gasped. She spun around to see her mom and dad dashing across the track to Phil. The other jockeys had pulled up and were trotting back down the track.

"Yes, but Phil needs help first," said Mark. He ran over to the Range Rover, flung open the driver's door, and grabbed the first aid kit from the glove compartment.

Mandy looked around in desperation. She saw Gary Hart trotting Jackdaw's Lad over toward the Range Rover. The big chestnut looked more upset than ever. He snorted nervously and thrashed his head up and down as he pranced sideways. Despite the cold wind, sweat foamed on his neck and ran down his front legs in thick streams.

Mark signaled to Gary to get his attention. "Do you think you can go after Bright Spark?" he called.

Gary looked at the hedge and shook his head. "I doubt it. Jack's way too stirred up. And anyway, that hedge is too dangerous to jump in cold blood."

Mandy felt Parsley wriggling inside her jacket. "You want your friend, don't you?" she said, putting the little dog on the ground.

Parsley ran straight to Jackdaw's Lad and stood up on her hind legs. She gave a short bark, and the chestnut tossed his head, scattering sticky white foam over the little terrier. Mark loosened the reins, and Jackdaw's Lad stretched down until he and the little dog were touching noses. Parsley licked her friend's face enthusiastically. Jackdaw's Lad flicked his ears and snorted again, already looking much calmer.

"That's incredible," said Mandy. "Parsley has calmed him down."

Mandy looked across the track to where her mom and dad were crouching down beside Phil. Dr. Adam was shining the small flashlight that he carried on his keyring into Phil's eyes.

Mandy's mom stood up and came running across the

track. "We'll have to get Phil to a hospital," she said. "He has a bump on the head, and we think he's broken his wrist."

"Should I call an ambulance?" asked Mark.

"It might take awhile to get here," said Dr. Emily. "It'll be better if you drive him there in the Range Rover."

"OK," said Mark. "I'll come and give you a hand."

"What about Bright Spark?" Mandy called as Mark ran across the track with Dr. Emily. "I could try to catch him."

Mark said something in reply, but his words were swallowed by the wind.

Mandy felt utterly helpless. With everyone busy handling horses or seeing to Phil, there were no spare hands for Bright Spark. What if he was hurt, like Phil? In a flash, Mandy made up her mind. "I'm going to get him," she said to James.

"I'll help you," James offered, charging after her.

They ran along the hedge, searching for a gap they could squeeze through.

"Over here," shouted James, dropping to his knees and pushing his way through a small hole at the bottom of the bushes.

Mandy tucked in her head and scrambled behind James, twigs scratching her face and her hands muddied by the damp earth. She stood up on the other side and was brushing the soil off her knees when she spotted a familiar white blaze through the trees.

"There he is," she whispered to James.

Bright Spark pricked up his ears and looked at them, his eyes still wide with fright. Mandy saw that the saddle had slipped around on his back so that it hung halfway down his side, while the broken reins dangled loosely in front of him. "I hope he doesn't suddenly bolt and trip himself up," she remarked.

Bright Spark lowered his head and nervously began to snatch at the grass. Mandy and James crept forward. Suddenly, a twig snapped under James's foot. Bright Spark's head shot up, and he stamped the ground with one hoof, the muscles on his shoulder twitching.

Mandy and James stood very still.

"It's OK," said Mandy in a soft, soothing voice. Bright Spark turned toward her with a jump and stared at her. "We've come to help you," Mandy continued, stretching out one hand and taking a few steps toward the horse.

Bright Spark eyed her suspiciously and stepped backward.

"Maybe I should circle around and approach from the other side," whispered James.

"Good idea," said Mandy. Out of the corner of her eye, she saw James doubling back and picking his way around the edge of the grove.

Mandy went forward inch by inch. "Here, boy," she mumured, keeping her hand stretched out. She wished she'd brought some alfalfa cubes with her. *Don't bolt*, she silently begged the thoroughbred. She was terrified that he would injure himself on the trees or trip on a root.

Bright Spark snorted and took another step backward. Mandy waited, then went forward again, saying softly, "Don't worry, Bright Spark. I won't hurt you."

This time, Bright Spark kept still. Mandy edged closer and closer. "There," she said as she picked up the broken reins. She half expected Bright Spark to rear and go charging off, but he stood calmly in front of her. "Good boy." She praised the startled horse and stroked his taut neck.

Bright Spark bent his head to sniff her pockets.

"Oh, I'm sorry," Mandy said. "I don't have any treats with me."

"I do," came James's voice from behind a nearby tree. He stepped out, holding a small rosy apple in one hand.

"Where on earth did you get that?" Mandy asked him.

"Here, in the grove," smiled James. "There's an apple tree over there, and it had just one apple on it!" He offered it to Bright Spark, who crunched it noisily.

"There, that helps, doesn't it?" Mandy said, stroking the horse's shoulder. "Are you ready to go back now?"

Holding the reins firmly and with James walking beside her, Mandy led Bright Spark through the trees and along the hedge until they found a gateway on the other side of the grove. They went through the gate and followed the edges of the trees back to the track.

Gary came running toward them as soon as they appeared at the corner of the wood. "Good job," he called out to them. "I was just coming to help."

"Where's Jackdaw's Lad?" Mandy asked.

"One of the other jockeys is holding him for me," answered Gary. "With Parsley there, he's as cool as a cucumber." He offered to take the reins from Mandy.

"It's OK," Mandy said, reaching up to smooth Bright Spark's mane. "I think he trusts me now."

They walked toward the Range Rover. On the other side of the railings, the rest of the jockeys had dismounted and were anxiously watching while Dr. Emily and Dr. Adam tended to Phil. Mandy watched her dad and Mark kneel down on either side of the injured boy and ease his arms onto their shoulders. With Phil supported between them, the two men slowly stood up and helped him across the track. Dr. Emily followed them, carrying Phil's cap.

Looking very groggy, Phil leaned against Dr. Adam while Mark opened the back door of the Range Rover. Phil stared blankly at the six horses. Then, as Mandy's dad was guiding him to the car door, he stiffened and opened his eyes wide. "Bright Spark," he muttered in a shaky voice. "Is he OK?"

"I'll check him over now," Dr. Emily offered. She walked over to where Mandy was holding the race-horse.

"He seems fine. He walked back here quite easily," Mandy told her mom.

"I want to have a look at him," Phil insisted.

Dr. Adam rested one hand on his shoulder. "Relax, Phil," he said. "Everything's under control."

Dr. Emily patted Bright Spark's neck, then smiled re-assuringly at Phil. "No serious injuries," she announced. "Just a few scratches from jumping the hedge."

"So he'll be racing on the day after Christmas?" asked Phil.

"I don't see why not," Dr. Emily assured him.

"Oh. Right," said Phil in a flat, faint voice.

Dr. Adam and Mark eased Phil into the Range Rover.

"It's going to be a tight squeeze on the ride back down," observed Mark.

"Don't worry about us," Dr. Adam told him. "You go on with Phil. We'll walk back with the others."

"Thanks," said Mark. "That means I can go straight to the hospital." He got a small blanket from the back of the vehicle and tucked it over Phil's knees. "Can you remember what actually happened at the last jump?" he asked.

Phil shook his head. "Only that Bright Spark was going too fast and that I had to check him."

Mark nodded. "Yes, that's what I thought." He carefully shut the back door, making sure not to jolt Phil.

Still looking very dazed, the stable boy slumped against the window and stared out at the other jockeys, who were mounting their horses to ride them back down to the training yard.

"Would you like us to lead Bright Spark back to the yard?" Mandy asked Mark.

"I don't know," the trainer said hesitantly. "I was going to ask Gary to lead him from Jackdaw's Lad. Bright Spark's a strong horse. He could easily pull away from you."

"Don't worry about that," Dr. Adam said. "Emily and I will make sure your horse gets back safely."

"That's very kind of you," said Mark, sounding relieved. He climbed into the Range Rover and, after checking once more that Phil was comfortable, drove slowly across the field toward the road.

It was a somber procession that wound down the hill toward the training yard. The jockeys rode in silence, their shoulders hunched against the wind. Mandy thought they were probably worried about Phil's injuries. Parsley, however, was as lively as ever. She scampered along next to Jackdaw's Lad, stopping every now and then to investigate a smell in the hedge with her long white nose.

The Hopes and James followed the rest of the racehorses with Bright Spark. Mandy held the horse's reins and walked next to his shoulder, letting Bright Spark choose his own pace, while James kept close to the thoroughbred's head, one hand resting on his neck. Her parents walked behind.

They were in sight of the stables when the big black clouds that had been gathering all morning suddenly broke. Huge drops of rain pelted down, quickly drenching everyone. The jockeys urged their horses into a trot, and soon they were all way ahead of Bright Spark.

"Pity we can't go any faster," said Mandy. She didn't think it would be a good idea to run down a hill with a racehorse in tow, especially one who had just had a nerve-racking experience. She noticed Bright Spark put his ears back nervously and roll his eyes as a gust of wind sent icy rain spattering against his haunches. "He doesn't look as if he's enjoying this much," she observed, tightening her grip on the slippery reins.

Dr. Adam came up beside Mandy. He ran one hand down the horse's shoulder and spoke soothingly to him.

"It's only rain. It won't hurt you, and you'll soon be inside your warm, dry stall."

Bright Spark kept going, but Mandy could tell he was unhappy, with his ears pinned back and his tail tucked into his hindquarters.

At last, with their clothes drenched and their shoes heavy with mud, they all trailed into the yard. Mandy's blond hair clung to her face in thick damp strands, while Bright Spark's coat was shiny and slippery from the rain. James could hardly see through his wet glasses, and he took them off to wipe them.

The other stable boys had already led their horses into the stalls and were unsaddling them.

"Do you think we should untack Bright Spark and rub him down?" Mandy asked, conscious that the horse must be as uncomfortable as she was.

"That's probably not necessary. There's bound to be a groom waiting for him," said Dr. Emily. "I think you should just take him to his stall."

"We'll wait for you and James in the car," said Mandy's dad. "I think the stable boys have enough on their plate without us getting in the way. So don't hang around the stall too long once the groom's taken over."

Mandy couldn't help feeling disappointed. She would have loved to help settle Bright Spark into his stall with a warm blanket and a fresh hay net. She reached up to stroke the white blaze on his face. "I guess we won't be seeing you again until the day after Christmas," she said. The horse nuzzled her fingers and snorted as if he were impatient to go inside. "OK, let's get you in your stall," said Mandy, and she let Bright Spark pick his way across the rain-slicked cobbles.

A blond stable girl came up as they pushed open the stall door. "Hi there," she said. "I'm Hayley. Gary told me about Phil's accident." She took the reins from Mandy. "Thanks for bringing him down." She led Bright Spark into the stall and started to untack him. Mandy and James stood just inside the door and watched her.

"What exactly happened?" asked Hayley, heaving the saddle off Bright Spark's back.

"They were doing really well," Mandy explained, "until Bright Spark met a fence on the wrong stride."

Hayley looked over her shoulder at Mandy and frowned. "That's really odd," she said as she picked up a brush and ran it down the horse's neck. "He's never done anything like that before. Mark will tell you that he's probably one of the most careful jumpers we've ever had."

"Phil said he had to check him because he was going too fast," James put in.

Hayley shook her head. "That sounds like bad luck. I expect Phil was very disappointed. He used to work at the same yard that Bright Spark came from, so he's known that horse longer than anyone." She tossed the brush into a plastic box just outside, then leaned against the door and studied Bright Spark. "It wasn't raining at the time, was it?" she asked.

"No, why?" said James.

Hayley grinned regretfully. "Like a lot of thin-skinned thoroughbreds, Sparky's well known for hating the rain. Sometimes we can't even persuade him to come out of his stall if it's raining."

"He didn't seem that bad when we were coming down the hill," Mandy pointed out. "It rained quite hard then. He flattened his ears and tucked in his tail, but he kept walking."

Hayley looked pleased. "Maybe he's growing out of his old habits," she said, following Mandy out. "That's something to cheer up poor Phil!"

That evening, back at Animal Ark, Mandy tried to watch TV with her mom and dad, but she couldn't concentrate. "Poor Phil." She sighed aloud during a commercial break. "I hope he's all right."

"I'm sure he'll be fine," said Dr. Adam, throwing another log on the fire.

"But he looked terrible when Mark drove him away,"

Mandy persisted. "And he was so worried about Bright Spark. He really loves that horse."

"Unfortunately, having a fall is something of an occupational hazard for jockeys," Dr. Emily warned.

"I think we should phone to find out how he is," Mandy said. "Dad, I'm sure Mark wouldn't mind."

"That means you want me to do it," said her dad, grinning and poking the log into place.

Mandy smiled back. "Yes, please. Otherwise I'll probably be awake all night worrying about him."

Dr. Adam went into the hall and phoned the trainer. Mandy stood in the doorway and listened.

"So? How is he?" she demanded when her dad put the phone down.

Dr. Adam smiled. "Mark says he's doing well and should be back at work in a week, although his wrist will be in a cast for a few weeks."

"I guess that means he won't be riding for quite a while," said Mandy.

"That's right," agreed Dr. Adam, going back into the living room and stretching out on the sofa. "But when you think about it, he's lucky to have come off so lightly. That was a bad fall."

Mandy nodded slowly. Replaying the events in slow motion in her mind, she pictured Bright Spark stumbling over the fence and crashing to the ground. Bright Spark could easily have landed on Phil, or Phil could have broken more serious bones than his wrist. She winced. "Maybe you're right, Dad," she agreed. "It could have been a lot worse."

# *Four*

"It was really dramatic," Mandy told Mrs. McFarlane. "One moment, the horses were jumping smoothly over the hurdles, then suddenly they were all over the place and Phil was lying on the ground under all those hooves."

"That's steeplechase for you," said the postmistress, tearing off some stamps and passing them to Mandy across the post office counter. "Just think of the Grand National and how many jockeys and horses fall."

It was the following Saturday morning, and Mandy and James were mailing their Christmas cards. James licked a stamp and put it on an envelope addressed to

Hare Hill. Inside was a card for Mark, Phil, and Bright Spark. "You can understand accidents happening when the horses are really racing," said James, pressing the stamp down with his fist. "But not when they're just practicing. I mean, Mark said they weren't even going full speed."

The doorbell jangled as another customer came in. It was Wilfred Bennet, a kind elderly man who had once owned Welford Riding Stables. Even though he had retired, he used his mare, Matty, to give rides to campers at the Rose of Yorkshire Campsite. Wilfred walked across to the counter, taking off his cap and smoothing down his white hair.

"Good morning, Mr. Bennet," said Mandy.

The old man nodded. "Morning," he said, putting a package on the counter.

"Mandy and James have just been telling me about an accident they saw last Sunday," said Mrs. McFarlane. She opened the cash register to give Wilfred his change.

Wilfred put the money in his pocket. "What kind of accident?" he asked.

Mandy explained again what had happened on the course.

The old man listened closely. "Bright Spark, you say?" he remarked when Mandy had finished. "I know that horse. He's been in quite a few local races. A first-rate jumper, that one. And as solid as a rock, except when it rains."

"Yes, one of the grooms told us he didn't like getting wet," said James.

Wilfred thought a moment. "Perhaps it was the rain that knocked him off his stride," he said.

"But it didn't start raining until after the accident," James pointed out. "When we were walking him back to Hare Hill."

"And he wasn't all that troubled by it even then," Mandy added.

Wilfred looked thoughtful. "So Bright Spark's at Hare Hill now, is he? That's one for the books. I never thought his previous owner would sell him."

"Who was that?" Mandy asked.

"Bob Fidler," the old man told her. He folded his arms and frowned. "Actually, now that I think of it, I'd heard that Fidler's yard was having a few money problems. Perhaps Bob sold some of his own horses to keep going," he said, his voice trailing away as he stared out the window with a wistful look on his face.

Mandy felt a pang of sympathy as she imagined what was going through Wilfred's mind. Wilfred had once been in financial trouble, too. He'd had to sell his riding stable to a farmer named Sam Western who had turned the land into a campsite. Even though Wilfred still lived nearby with Matty, it couldn't be the same as having his own yard full of horses.

Wilfred gave himself a shake and turned to the others. He donned his cap and went toward the door. "Have a great Christmas, all of you," he said, going outside.

"Same to you," said James as he and Mandy followed Wilfred out.

Blackie was waiting for them at the bottom of the steps. Dogs weren't allowed in the post office, so James always left the Labrador tied to the railing while he went inside.

Blackie was delighted to see them. He thumped his tail on the ground and squirmed excitedly while James untied him.

"Down, boy," said James sternly as Blackie jumped up and licked his face.

But Blackie ignored his owner and bounced up and down, almost knocking James off his feet. "Will you ever grow up?" James sighed, pushing Blackie down for the fifth time.

"Probably in about ten years," Mandy said, laughing.

The two friends dropped their cards into the mailbox and started for home. They parted at the crossroads. James was playing football that afternoon while Mandy would be busy with her regular duties at Animal Ark, feeding the patients in the residential unit and cleaning out their cages.

"See you tomorrow night," Mandy called over her shoulder as she started up the road to Animal Ark. "Dad says we'll pick you up at about half-past five."

To Mandy's delight, the Hopes and James were going back to Hare Hill the next evening. Mark Sheldon had phoned during the week to invite them all to a pre-Christmas gathering to thank them for their help after Phil's accident. He'd also told them that Phil had been discharged from the hospital and was feeling a lot better, even though his wrist was still in a cast.

Arriving at the clinic five minutes later, Mandy found it full of animals and their owners. With just a week to go before Christmas, a lot of people were going away, and they wanted to make sure their pets were in good health before they took them to boarding kennels.

"It's like a railroad station in here," Mandy joked to the receptionist, Jean Knox. All the seats were taken by clients waiting their turn. Three dogs lay on the floor at their owner's feet, while a raucous Amazon parrot sat squawking in his cage. There were also several carrying cases, and when Mandy peered through the wire doors she counted two cats, a rabbit, and a pair of guinea pigs.

Jean was hunting around on her desk, looking rather flustered. "Where are my glasses?" she muttered.

"Er, on their chain, around your neck," said Simon, the clinic's nurse, grinning as he came in from an examining room with a pile of patients' files in his arms. The tall, blond man winked at Mandy, who grinned back at him.

Jean fumbled for her glasses and put them on. "Thank you, Simon," she said as he put the files on her desk, then went back to the examining room. Jean looked down at the files with dismay. "I don't know when I'll get the chance to put those away, with all the phone calls and the payments and people pouring in all the time." She sighed.

"I'll help you," Mandy offered. She opened a drawer in the filing cabinet and started to put away the files while Jean prepared the bill for a man who had brought his cat for an inoculation.

The phone rang. Jean ignored it, concentrating instead on the numbers she was adding up.

"I'll get it," Mandy said, and reached for the receiver. "Animal Ark," she greeted the caller. "May I help you?"

A booming voice answered her. "Ah, yes. Is that Amanda?" It was Mrs. Ponsonby, the winner of the free vet check.

Mandy's heart sank. Mrs. Ponsonby certainly knew how to choose her timing! *She can't want to claim her prize now*, Mandy thought, looking around at all the patients. She saw her mom usher a little boy and two small dogs into the examining room just as the front door opened to admit another family with a budgie in a cage.

"Yes. This is Mandy speaking," she said into the receiver. "Hello, Mrs. Ponsonby."

"Hello, dear. Now the thing is, we're having a dreadful time up here," announced Mrs. Ponsonby. "The central heating's out of order so we're all freezing."

Mandy guessed that Mrs. Ponsonby wasn't exaggerating. Bleakfell Hall, where Mrs. Ponsonby lived, was a big, drafty Victorian mansion with enormous rooms and high ceilings. It would be very uncomfortable with no heating. "It must be awful," Mandy sympathized.

"Yes. Such a nuisance," said Mrs. Ponsonby. "The plumber can't come to fix the boiler until tomorrow."

Mandy was beginning to feel impatient.

"It's very hard on my two precious poppets," continued Mrs. Ponsonby.

"You mean Pandora and Toby?" Mandy asked.

"Of course. Darling Pandora's particularly upset today," said Mrs. Ponsonby. "She simply wasn't herself when she woke up this morning. And she's drinking an awful lot — much more than normal. I do believe she's coming down with something."

So that's what it was all about! Mandy suspected that Mrs. Ponsonby was using the broken furnace as an excuse to have her dogs checked over.

"You know, that free checkup is valid for as long as you like," Mandy pointed out as patiently as she could. "You don't have to use it right away. Mom and Dad are very busy at the moment because of Christmas."

Mrs. Ponsonby ignored Mandy's remark. "The poor dog is just so lethargic. She's lying in a heap, panting.

And as I told you, she's dreadfully thirsty," complained the fussy owner.

Mandy sighed to herself. "Have you changed her diet at all?" she asked, hoping she could find a sensible reason for Pandora's behavior.

"No. Not at all," replied Mrs. Ponsonby. And that's the other thing. She's completely lost her appetite. She wouldn't even eat her chicken pâté this morning!"

*Chicken pâté!* Mandy exclaimed silently. Pandora would probably much rather have some ordinary dog food. But instead of voicing her opinion, she asked, "How much exercise is she getting?" While she spoke, she held the phone between her ear and shoulder so that she could continue to put the files away.

"She hasn't had much lately because I don't like her to get too cold," Mrs. Ponsonby admitted.

"I never let her or Toby out of my sight," she continued. "But that's not the issue. What is important is that Pandora's not herself. She ought to be seen by your parents at once."

"What is she doing right now?" Mandy asked. She waved at her dad who had come to call his next patient. Pointing to the phone, she made a face and mouthed, *Mrs. Ponsonby.*

Her dad put on a look of mock terror, then hurried

back into his examining room ahead of a young boy who was carrying a basket of guinea pigs.

"Right now, she's curled up on my lap," said Mrs. Ponsonby. "But I really think I should bring her in."

Mandy thought quickly. Without regular exercise, and being cuddled on Mrs. Ponsonby's ample lap, Pandora was bound to be feeling hot and lazy!

"You can bring her in by all means," Mandy said, reaching for the blue appointment book on the desk and running her finger down the page. There wasn't a single available time slot that day. "But we're chockablock today, I'm afraid, Mrs. Ponsonby. You can come in on Monday, though."

There was a sigh and a pause, then Mrs. Ponsonby said, "Are you sure you can't just squeeze us in between patients?"

Mandy knew that her mom and dad would always make room for an emergency. But knowing Mrs. Ponsonby, she thought it was unlikely that Pandora was in critical condition. "We're really busier than we can handle," she said quite truthfully as two more people came in with a large German shepherd. "But I'll put you down for the first appointment on Monday morning." She picked up a pen and waited for Mrs. Ponsonby to answer.

"I suppose that will have to do," Mrs. Ponsonby said.

"Pandora will be fine." Mandy hoped she sounded re-assuring. "Good-bye, Mrs. Ponsonby." She put the phone back on the base and wrote Mrs. Ponsonby's name in the appointment book.

"What was that all about?" asked Jean Knox.

"Not much — as usual." Mandy grinned, sliding the book back to Jean. "There's no heat up at Bleakfell Hall. Pandora's hot and thirsty." She stopped short. Hot and thirsty! With no heating? "That can't be right." She gasped out loud. Ignoring the curious looks of everyone in the reception room, she charged over to her mom's examining room and burst inside.

Mrs. Hope was examining a fat tabby cat. She looked up at Mandy in surprise. "Is there something wrong, dear?"

"It's Pandora," Mandy blurted out. "I think she's seri-ously ill."

# *Five*

"What do you think it could be?" Mandy asked her mom five minutes later as they sped down the lane on their way to Bleakfell Hall. As soon as Mandy described Pandora's symptoms, Dr. Emily had sprung into action. The Pekingese needed to be seen immediately. Leaving Dr. Adam and Simon to see the rest of the patients, Dr. Emily had grabbed her vet's bag and hurried out to the garage, with Mandy running to keep up.

Dr. Emily frowned as she turned onto the main road. "I'm not sure without seeing Pandora first, but it could be any of a number of acute infections," she said.

"At first I thought Mrs. Ponsonby was exaggerating as usual," Mandy admitted guiltily.

Dr. Emily glanced at her with understanding. "I'd probably have jumped to the same conclusion. Mrs. Ponsonby's made a fuss about her dogs' health so many times now, it's hard to know when to take her seriously. But you're right about Pandora's symptoms — they do sound serious."

Leaving the village, they turned onto a narrow road and crossed a river, then continued for a few miles before coming to a wrought-iron gate. Mandy jumped out to open it before they drove up the long gravel driveway.

"I just hope we're in time," she said breathlessly, leaning forward in her seat as they approached the gray stone mansion.

They pulled up in front of the house and jumped out to run up the steps.

"Answer the door, someone," Mandy muttered anxiously as she pressed the old-fashioned bell beside the massive oak front door. She heard the bell echoing through the house, quickly followed by an excited bark that she recognized as Toby's. Next came the sound of heavy footsteps crossing the hall. A heavy bolt was slid aside and the door swung open.

"Emily and Mandy!" exclaimed Mrs. Ponsonby when she saw them standing on the top step. "I thought you were very busy at Animal Ark."

"We are," Mandy said. "But we were worried about Pandora, after what you told us."

"I think she could be very ill," Dr. Emily explained.

"Oh, my!" said Mrs. Ponsonby, wringing her hands. "Come in, hurry."

She led them across the wood-paneled hall and into the living room. A huge fire crackled in the grate but did little to warm up the big, high-ceilinged room. Toby was curled up in his basket in front of the fire, but he jumped up and ran over to greet them as they came in. Mandy patted him on the head and then followed her mom and Mrs. Ponsonby across the room to an enormous sofa.

"Here she is, the poor baby," said Mrs. Ponsonby.

The silky-haired little dog lay panting on a cushion at one end of the sofa. Her head drooped between her front paws, and her eyes were half closed.

Mandy knelt down next to her and gently smoothed her light brown coat. "You do look sick," she murmured, looking at the tiny face, which seemed more crumpled than ever. "But Mom's here. She'll take care of you."

The Pekingese gazed blankly at Mandy as if she didn't even recognize her.

Whimpering, Toby put his front paws up on the sofa, then licked Pandora's face. But Pandora didn't respond. Mandy put an arm around the dog and nudged him off the sofa. "She probably just wants to be left alone," she said to Toby.

Dr. Emily took a stethoscope and thermometer out of her bag. She checked Pandora's heart rate and breathing and took her temperature. "Mmm. Higher than normal," she said. Gently, she turned the Peke onto her side. "Hold her like that for me while I examine her tummy, please," she asked Mandy.

Mandy laid one hand on Pandora's head and the other on her heaving rib cage while Dr. Emily crouched down next to the sofa and palpated the dog's tummy. Pandora squirmed and whimpered.

"Poor girl. That hurts, doesn't it?" Mandy said, stroking Pandora's head.

"When did this start?" Dr. Emily asked Mrs. Ponsonby.

"Well, she's been looking strange and drinking more than usual for about two days," answered Mrs. Ponsonby. "Do you think she has a stomach infection?"

Dr. Emily stood up. "No. Far from it. Pandora's acutely ill. I think she has something called pyometra."

"Oh, my goodness! What's that?" cried Mrs. Ponsonby, clutching her hands to her chest.

"A very serious infection," explained Dr. Emily. She took off her stethoscope and put it in her bag. "Pandora needs emergency surgery," she announced, snapping the bag shut.

"Surgery!" Mrs. Ponsonby gasped, her double chin wobbling. "Are you sure?"

"I'm afraid so," said Dr. Emily. "It's her only hope."

Mrs. Ponsonby's face turned white. "You mean, she could . . . die?" she whispered hoarsely, staring down at her beloved dog.

"There is a risk, yes," confirmed Dr. Emily. "But if we operate today, we might just be able to save her."

"Just be able to save her?" echoed Mrs. Ponsonby in a small, weak voice.

Mandy put a hand on Mrs. Ponsonby's arm. "Pandora will be fine, you'll see." But even though she tried to sound confident, Mandy had seen a few cases of pyometra before and knew just how life threatening the disease was.

"We'll operate as soon as we get her back to Animal Ark," said Dr. Emily, picking up her bag while Mandy carefully scooped Pandora into her arms.

Promising to keep Mrs. Ponsonby well informed,

Mandy and her mom drove hastily away, leaving the distraught woman watching them from the front steps. Toby was standing next to her, his head cocked to one side as if he were trying to figure out why Pandora was being taken away.

Back at Animal Ark, all was quiet. The last patients had been seen, and Dr. Adam had left to do a house call at a farm on the moor. Simon was just about to go home as Mandy and her mom hurried into the clinic.

"What's this?" the nurse asked when he saw Pandora lying limply in Mandy's arms.

"Acute pyometra," Mandy told him. "Mom's going to operate."

Simon immediately took off his jacket and hung it on a peg behind the door. "In that case, I'll give you a hand," he said.

Mandy carried Pandora into the operating room and spoke soothingly to her while her mom and Simon scrubbed up.

Dr. Emily pulled on her sterile gown and a pair of latex gloves, then prepared the anesthetic while Simon put up an IV. "OK, Pandora," he said, gently taking the dog from Mandy and putting her on the table. "Let's get you fixed up."

The phone started to ring out in the waiting room.

"Could you answer it please, Mandy?" asked Dr. Emily.

Even before she picked up the receiver, Mandy guessed that the caller would be Mrs. Ponsonby.

"How's Pandora?" came the anxious question.

"She's just gone into the operating room," Mandy told her. "We'll let you know the moment she comes around."

Half an hour later, Mandy's mother called Mrs. Ponsonby back. "Pandora's come through the operation," she told her.

Standing close to her, Mandy was able to hear Mrs. Ponsonby's relieved response.

"Oh, thank heavens!" said Mrs. Ponsonby over the phone. "When can I pick her up?"

"Not for a while, I'm afraid," replied Dr. Emily. "We'll need to keep a close watch on her for the next twenty-four hours."

Mrs. Ponsonby said something that Mandy couldn't hear, and Dr. Emily said, "No, I don't think you should visit her just yet, if you don't mind. She needs to be kept very quiet, and she might get too excited if she sees you. But we'll let you know as soon as she's well enough for you to visit."

Dr. Emily hung up, and she and Mandy went to check on Pandora once more before going into the cottage for supper.

Attached to an IV, Pandora lay utterly still in a cage in the residential unit. Her tummy had been shaved for the operation, and the black stitches stood out sharply against her tender pink skin.

"Poor little thing," murmured Mandy, lightly petting Pandora's head with one finger. "Do you think she'll be better in time for Christmas?"

"I hope so," replied her mom, rubbing her eyes in exhaustion. It had been a long day, and Dr. Emily had barely had a break since early that morning. "But the next twelve hours or so will be critical."

"You're going to make it, Pandora," Mandy promised softly, then followed her mom out of the unit, hoping more than anything else that she was right.

"Look! Pandora's bounced back really quickly," Mandy told James late the next afternoon when he climbed into the Land Rover next to her. The Hopes had stopped to pick him up on their way to Hare Hill. Pandora was sitting on Mandy's lap, looking out the window.

"You're a brave little thing," Mandy said, caressing the Peke's silken ears. "And much tougher than you look."

The operation had been a success, and the little dog was well enough to go home. To Mrs. Ponsonby's delight, the Hopes were dropping Pandora at Bleakfell Hall on their way to the stables.

"Yes, she must be really tough," said James to Mandy as he stroked Pandora's back. "When you phoned me yesterday and said how ill she was, I thought I'd never see her again. I bet Mrs. Ponsonby's pleased."

"She's more than that," said Dr. Adam. "And knowing her, there'll be a reception committee for Pandora when we arrive."

As Mandy's dad had predicted, Mrs. Ponsonby was waiting for them at the front door, with Toby at her side.

The moment she saw the Land Rover, she bustled down the steps, a broad smile on her face. "Pandora, darling," she cried, flinging open her arms as Mandy climbed out with the Peke, "come to Mommy!" She took Pandora from Mandy and held her in her arms as if she were made of porcelain. "Are you all better now, sweetheart?" she crooned.

"You'll have to keep her quiet for the next few days," said Dr. Emily, climbing out of the Land Rover. She handed Mrs. Ponsonby a bottle of antibiotic pills. "And give her one of these three times a day. We don't want any secondary infections setting in."

"Thank you all so much," said Mrs. Ponsonby, beaming. "I can't tell you how much this dog means to me. If anything had happened to her — " She stopped and shook her head slowly, then turned to Mandy. "But thanks to your quick thinking, she's safe and sound."

"I didn't do much," Mandy said modestly.

"Oh, but you did," insisted Mrs. Ponsonby. "You were the one who realized that she was in danger."

Mandy felt uncomfortable. She could hardly admit that she hadn't taken Mrs. Ponsonby's fears seriously at first. "I just put two and two together," she said.

"And that's exactly why you'll make a good vet some day," Dr. Adam said, starting the engine again. "Good-bye, Mrs. Ponsonby. Call us at once if you have any worries about Pandora."

The Hopes and James arrived at Hare Hill after dark to find the place looking very festive. Even from a distance, Mandy could see that lots of twinkling lights had been strung on the trees that lined the driveway. Tiny silver lights hung from the eaves of the stables, and a huge Christmas tree with multicolored bulbs took pride of place in the middle of the yard.

Mark had heard them arriving and came out to meet them. He lived in a cozy cottage next to the stables, but he led them straight to the imposing manor house at the far side of a magnificent sweep of gravel drive. "My mother wants to meet you all as well," he explained. "She's hosting the party tonight."

Grace Sheldon was waiting for them in her enormous firelit living room. She was a tall, elegant woman with short golden-brown hair, almost the same color as Jackdaw's Lad's coat, Mandy realized.

"We're very grateful for all your help last Sunday," Mrs. Sheldon said in greeting them, shaking everyone's hand.

"Thank goodness there were no permanent injuries," said Dr. Emily, accepting a glass of fruit punch from a black-uniformed butler.

"Yes. Phil's much better, and Bright Spark seems none the worse for his little expedition into the woods," smiled Mark. "We'll go to see him later if you like." He poured some fruit punch for Mandy and James. "I thought it was very brave of the two of you to go after him. A nervous racehorse isn't easy to control."

"He was as good as gold," Mandy said. She was looking at a series of framed photographs of racehorses above the mantelpiece. "Are these all your horses?" she asked Mark.

"They were my father's," Mark told her. "He was a very successful racehorse trainer." He pointed to a photograph of a black horse flying over a high brush fence at least two lengths ahead of the rest of the field. "That's Knight's Dance, one of his most famous horses, competing in the Grand National. He won it that year." A warm look came into his eyes. "That was a horse in a million. He and I were really close."

"Yes. You used to say you could tell what he was thinking," Mrs. Sheldon reminded Mark. She looked up at the famous horse. "He won the Grand National the following year, too," she said proudly. "It's the kind of form we're hoping Bright Spark will develop."

"Well, let's hope he doesn't repeat his mistake at the hurdle when he's racing on the day after Christmas," said Mark. He raised his glass and paused while every-one else lifted theirs. "To Bright Spark. Good luck in his first race for Hare Hill," he said.

"To Bright Spark," Mandy echoed, catching James's eye and grinning.

"And to his temporary owners." Mrs. Sheldon smiled.

"I'll drink to that," said Dr. Adam, chuckling.

Mark finished his punch, then asked Mandy and James if they'd like to go with him on his evening rounds to check the horses.

"Yes, please," Mandy said, downing her spicy punch.

It was a still, crisp evening, and Mandy could hear one or two horses snorting in their stables as they ap-proached the well-lit yard. They walked down the row of box stalls, with Mark stopping to look at each horse and speak to the head groom about feed or training. When they came to the stall belonging to Jackdaw's Lad, Mandy peered in over the half door. Unlike the other horses, whose feed was placed in mangers, the chestnut racehorse had his nose in a rubber bucket on the floor.

"Enjoying your supper?" Mandy asked softly.

"I wonder why his food is on the floor?" said James, sounding puzzled.

Jackdaw's Lad lifted his head and looked at them. He

blew a greeting down his nostrils, then turned to look behind him before burying his nose in the bucket again.

"It's like he's trying to tell us something," Mandy said.

"I think he was." James laughed. "Look there." He pointed to the manger at the back of the stall. There, curled up on a blanket, was a familiar tan-and-white shape. Parsley! "I guess that's why poor old Jackdaw's Lad has to eat off the floor!"

"Yes, you can see who's king around here," Mandy agreed, smiling.

They continued down the row to Bright Spark's stall. Mark opened the door and they all went inside. To Mandy's surprise, Phil was there. One arm was in a plaster cast, and he was grooming Bright Spark with his good hand, sweeping a soft brush in long, smooth strokes over the racehorse's gleaming coat. He had folded Bright Spark's stable blankets onto his quarters to keep him warm, and his pink face suggested he had been working for some time.

"Evening all," said the stable boy, glancing briefly at them.

"Hi," Mandy responded. She was really impressed by how devoted Phil was to Bright Spark. He was already back at work only days after his accident, and Bright Spark looked magnificent.

"Are you feeling better?" asked James.

Phil nodded. "Much better." He lifted his injured arm. "But this is slowing me up a lot. That's why I'm so late grooming Sparky."

"If it's too much for you, I can ask Hayley to help out," Mark offered.

"No. It's not too much," Phil said hurriedly. "I can manage, really I can. I don't mind being here late."

"Well, let me know if you change your mind," said Mark. "Oh, and I've arranged for Hayley to take over from you for the big race. With that broken wrist, it'll be difficult for you to look after Bright Spark at the track."

A look of disappointment clouded Phil's face, but he said nothing and continued brushing the horse.

Mandy reached out and stroked Bright Spark's neck. His coat felt smooth and soft, and his scratches had healed well. "You're lucky to have someone who cares so much for you," she murmured, running her fingers through his thick black mane.

"He's looking really good," observed James. "I bet he'll do well in the race. What do you think, Phil?"

Phil shrugged without stopping to look at them. Mandy thought he seemed even less enthusiastic about the race than before. *Maybe it's because he won't be there*, she told herself. Or could it be that Phil was worried that Bright Spark might fall again?

Mandy patted Bright Spark's shoulder. "I bet he'll sail over those jumps," she declared, trying to help Phil feel more positive about his horse. "And will be the first one past the finish line."

The horse snorted into his hay as if he agreed with her, but the dark expression on Phil's face didn't change.

# Six

On Christmas Day, Mandy and her parents popped in to see Pandora and Mrs. Ponsonby after church. Mrs. Ponsonby was normally a very enthusiastic member of the choir, but she hadn't turned up for the special Christmas service. Mandy suspected that Pandora might be the reason. "I hope Pandora's OK," she said uneasily as they drove through the gates to Bleakfell Hall.

"I'm sure she is," said Dr. Emily. "I spoke to Mrs. Ponsonby only two days ago and she said all was well."

"And if it wasn't we'd have heard about it by now," Dr. Adam added with a grin.

Mandy's fears vanished the moment Mrs. Ponsonby

opened the front door. Tucked under her owner's arm, Pandora gave a sharp yap and wagged her tail happily when she saw Mandy.

"You look as right as rain," Mandy said, petting the little dog.

"She's absolutely one hundred percent fit again," boomed Mrs. Ponsonby as she ushered the Hopes indoors. Toby scampered along next to them, holding a rubber ball in his mouth. He had a festive red ribbon tied to his collar, and Mandy was sure she could see some Christmas cake crumbs clinging to his muzzle.

Mandy bent down and prized the ball away from the mixed breed, then rolled it down the long passage. Toby galloped after it and returned in a flash, his claws clicking on the wooden floor, to drop the ball at Mandy's feet. "Is this your Christmas present?" Mandy asked him with a smile, picking the ball up.

Toby barked and Mandy sent the ball down the passage again, then followed her mom and dad and Mrs. Ponsonby into the living room.

"We were worried when we didn't see you at church," Dr. Emily said to Mrs. Ponsonby.

"I really ought to have been there," said Mrs. Ponsonby, setting Pandora down on a velvet cushion on the sofa. Toby galloped through the door, the ball in his mouth, and leaped onto the sofa next to Pandora. Mrs.

Ponsonby smiled affectionately at him, then continued, "But I simply couldn't leave Pandora so soon after her big operation. Could I, my darling?" she said, and bent stiffly to kiss the top of the Peke's head.

Mandy bit her lip to stop herself from laughing. Things were definitely back to normal at Bleakfell Hall! Mrs. Ponsonby was as fussy as ever, even though Pandora was well on the road to recovery.

"Would you like some coffee? Or," Mrs. Ponsonby looked at her watch, "a glass of milk?"

"Thank you, but no," said Dr. Emily. "We're not staying. We have a houseful for lunch, and they'll all be arriving shortly. We just stopped by to check on Pandora."

"That's very kind of you," said Mrs. Ponsonby, straightening the plaid bow she'd tied in Pandora's bangs. "I'm so very grateful to you all for taking such good care of her the other day."

"It's what we do," Dr. Adam said, smiling.

"No. That was exceptional," insisted Mrs. Ponsonby. "Quite beyond the call of duty to come tearing out here and then to operate so quickly." She took a box of chocolates off the mantlepiece and offered them around. She waited while Dr. Adam chose one wrapped in gold foil, then said, "In return for your kindness, there's something I'd like to do for you."

"That's not necessary — " began Dr. Adam, but Mrs. Ponsonby stopped him.

"I absolutely insist on doing you a favor," she said. "One good turn deserves another, you know." She put the lid on the chocolates, then gave them to Mandy. "You can take these, dear, for a start," she said. "I shouldn't be eating such things."

"Oh, thank you," Mandy said. "That's very kind of you."

But it seemed that Mrs. Ponsonby had something else in mind for her good deed. "I've been racking my brains thinking what I could do for you all," she said. "And then I remembered the prize you won in the raffle, Adam."

"Bright Spark?" Mandy asked.

Mrs. Ponsonby nodded. "It dawned on me that you might enjoy being driven to the racecourse to see him run. So, as long as you agree, I have arranged for my driver to pick you up in the Bentley tomorrow morning and take you to Lingwood Park."

"Oh, wow!" Mandy exclaimed enthusiastically, her eyes lighting up. "That will be awesome, Mrs. Ponsonby!" She grinned at her mom and dad. "Just wait till we tell James. He'll be thrilled."

"That's a lovely idea," Dr. Emily agreed.

"And it'll save us the trouble of having to find a parking place," added Dr. Adam. "Thank you, Mrs. Ponsonby. It's a very generous offer, and we'd love to take you up on it."

Mrs. Ponsonby beamed happily. "It's the least I can do."

A few minutes later, after wishing Mrs. Ponsonby and her dogs a merry Christmas, the Hopes climbed back into the Land Rover. "Of course," said Dr. Adam, looking over his shoulder at Mandy as he started the engine, "riding in a fancy Bentley means we'll have to dress a bit more carefully." He raised his eyebrows at her blue jeans.

Mandy laughed. "Look who's talking!" She leaned over and tugged at her dad's baggy brown corduroy pants. "I hope you weren't thinking of wearing those!"

"What do you mean?" said Dr. Adam, pretending to be offended. "They're very nice pants."

"Used to be," Dr. Emily corrected him with a chuckle.

"The car's here," Mandy called excitedly to her parents, hearing the sound of an engine. It was half-past ten the next morning, and Mandy and James were waiting in the hall for the Bentley to arrive. James had come over on his bike half an hour earlier.

"Be there in a sec," called Dr. Adam. "Just getting my binoculars."

Dr. Emily came into the hall, buttoning her coat just as the dark blue car drove by the Animal Ark sign and up the driveway to the front door. "Now that's what I call a car." She smiled, peering out the window at the sleek vehicle.

"Let's go," Mandy said eagerly. She pulled on her gloves and opened the door.

James grabbed his raincoat and went out after her. Dr. Emily waited for Mandy's dad to catch up, then she locked the door and followed the others down the front steps.

"Good morning," said the uniformed driver. "My name is Simmonds, and I'm your chauffeur for the day." His blue eyes twinkled as he opened the back door for them.

"Thank you," said Mandy, stepping into the luxurious car. She sank into the deep leather seat and stretched out her legs.

"This is cool," James said, sliding in next to her. "Imagine always going around in such a neat car."

"Well, you'd better not get too used to it," Mandy warned. "We'll be back on our bikes tomorrow."

"Yes. But they're fun, too," said James loyally.

"Until it rains," pointed out Dr. Emily, settling back in her seat while her husband climbed into the front seat next to the driver.

Mandy glanced anxiously out the window. "I hope it doesn't rain today," she said, crossing her fingers. Even though Bright Spark seemed to be getting over his dislike of the rain, the last thing she wanted was for him to be put to the test on race day! But the sky was blue and clear, with just a few fluffy white clouds on the horizon.

They arrived at Lingwood Park an hour later. Mark had arranged to meet them at the main gate, so Simmonds dropped them off, then went to find a space in the busy parking lot.

"What an amazing car," said Mark, handing them each a ticket for the members' enclosure.

"Only the best for Bright Spark's temporary owner." Dr. Adam grinned as he tied the scarlet tag onto the strap of his binoculars.

Mark waited while Dr. Emily went through the turnstile, then he pushed the revolving gate and followed her. "Whose car is it?" he asked.

"It belongs to a Pekingese named Pandora," Mandy joked as she went through a neighboring turnstile.

Mark looked stunned. "You're kidding."

"Not really," said James. He told Mark about Mrs. Ponsonby and her beloved dogs. "I bet she'll leave everything she owns to Pandora and Toby."

"You're probably right," said an amused Dr. Adam.

The race day had drawn a huge crowd. Wrapped up warmly against the cold, people bustled back and forth between the track and the restaurant or stood together in groups eagerly discussing the races.

"It's like Walton on market day," Mandy remarked to James as they threaded a path through the lines in front of the bookmakers' booths. Above them stood a small wooden grandstand overlooking the white-railed track. Already most of the seats in the stand had been taken by spectators, who sat closely studying the race card.

"Where are the horses?" Mandy asked, looking around. She wanted to wish Bright Spark and Gary good luck before their race.

"Ours are still on the way over in the van," explained Mark. "But they should be here any minute. Let's go to the stables to wait for them."

The horses waited before each race in temporary stabling at the back of the grandstand. There were dozens there already, some of them calmly looking out over the stall doors while others were being tacked up outside. Jockeys clad in brightly colored silks, with their caps tucked under their arms, stood in huddles talking to trainers and owners.

"This is great!" Mandy exclaimed, feeling herself caught up in the exciting prerace atmosphere. But at the same time, she was nervous. Bright Spark was entered for the second biggest race of the day. Would he have recovered from his fall by now?

"Ah, here they are," said Mark as a horse van with HARE HILL YARD painted on the side pulled up next to them.

Mandy looked up at the small windows near the roof and saw a row of horses' noses sniffing at the air. A human-sized door opened in the side of the van, and Hayley climbed out. "Hi, everyone," she said, then hurried around to the back to begin unloading the horses.

Mandy and James followed her and helped to lower the ramp. They stood well out of the way as the Hare Hill horses emerged one by one, led by their grooms.

"They look fantastic!" Mandy said, watching the racehorses step carefully down the ramp and onto the pavement. They looked immaculate in smart woolen blankets in the striking Hare Hill colors of red and gold, and with their coats polished to a glossy shine. One or two of them pranced in high spirits as if they could hardly wait to get to the track.

"Here comes Jackdaw's Lad," said James as the long-legged chestnut appeared at the top of the ramp. He tossed his head and looked around, then neighed loudly.

"Where's Parsley?" Mandy asked.

"There, in the driver's cab." James pointed.

The little white-faced terrier was standing up at the window, resting her front paws on the ledge. Her face was alive with excitement as she watched the horses circling.

"I don't suppose she's allowed out with all the horses," Mandy said to Mark.

"Not really," confirmed Mark. "Jackdaw's Lad loves her, but I think the other horses could find her a bit annoying!"

Bright Spark was the next to clatter down the ramp. Looking very calm, he stood with his ears pricked while the Hopes and James went over to see him.

Mandy ran her fingers through the horse's forelock. "Good luck, you gorgeous fellow. I know you're going to run your heart out for us and come home safely," she murmured, looking deep into his intelligent brown eyes.

The horse held her gaze for a few moments before turning to look at Dr. Adam, who was patting his neck.

"Now remember, Bright Spark." Dr. Adam smiled. "You're running for Animal Ark today. So let's see you soaring over those jumps and being first past the finish line."

Bright Spark stamped the ground and shook his head.

"Is that a yes or a no?" wondered James.

"It is a definite yes." Mandy grinned. "Isn't it, you lovely horse?" She stroked the white blaze on his face.

A sudden chilly gust of wind whipped around them, carrying with it a hint of rain. Bright Spark flinched, but Mandy was quick to reassure him. "You don't have to worry about rain anymore," she told him. "You know it won't hurt you. And anyway, with luck it won't rain until much later."

Dr. Emily tucked her scarf inside her coat. "Whatever the weather does, I'm sure Bright Spark and Gary will do their best," she said. "And at the end of the day, that's all that really counts."

"No, it isn't," protested Dr. Adam, smiling. "This is a race. You've got to be competitive, otherwise there's no point in taking part, is there?"

Mark laughed. "I'm with you there, Adam. And let me assure you, there isn't a more competitive jockey than

Gary Hart. With him in the saddle, Bright Spark's bound to do well."

"Now that's what I like to hear," said Dr. Adam.

Mark looked at his watch. "We'd better join my mother for lunch now. The first race is in half an hour."

Mandy gave Bright Spark a parting pat, then followed the others out of the stable yard and past the collecting ring to the grandstand. "When is Bright Spark running?" she asked, glancing over her shoulder. She could just see Hayley leading the horse to an empty stable, his hindquarters swaying elegantly under the gold-and-scarlet blanket.

"He's in the third race, at two o'clock," said Mark. "And Jackdaw's Lad is in the big race, which is the last one of the day."

Grace Sheldon was waiting for them in her private box at the top of the grandstand. It was a spacious room with a huge glass window overlooking the track. It felt comfortably warm after the bitter wind. At the far end of the box, a door opened onto a balcony so that people could stand outside to watch the horses streak past the finish line just below.

"Ah, there you all are," said Mrs. Sheldon. She was sitting in a comfortable chair, and a race card lay on her lap. "Perfect timing, too," she added as a waitress came in carrying a tray with two quiches and a bowl of salad.

There was a table in the center of the room with chairs around it. The smiling waitress set the food down on it, then left, saying she'd return with the dessert after the first race.

Mandy and James sat at the end of the table next to the window, where they had an uninterrupted view of the track and crowds below. The others sat down, too, and started their lunch.

"This looks delicious," said Dr. Emily appreciatively, helping herself to salad before passing the bowl to Mandy's dad. "A lovely change from Christmas left-overs!"

"Yes. And what a way to spend the day after Christmas," commented Dr. Adam. "Feasting sumptuously before cheering on our own horse in a steeplechase race."

Mandy speared a tiny tomato with her fork. "What does *steeplechase* actually mean?" she asked.

"Originally, back in the eighteenth century, gentlemen farmers used to race each other across country," Mrs. Sheldon explained, taking a glass of juice that Mark had poured for her. "Riders had to gallop at full tilt from one parish to the next, or from one church steeple to another, jumping whatever got in their way, like rivers and fences. So that's why racecourses today have hurdles and ditches."

Mandy caught James's eye and smiled. She liked the idea that the races today were part of a centuries-old tradition.

They'd just finished lunch when a voice came over the loudspeaker announcing that the horses for the first race were about to leave the parade ring.

Mandy pushed back her chair and hurried over to the window. Looking through her binoculars, she watched seven or eight thoroughbreds file out onto the track, then canter past the spectators toward the starting tape. "I like the gray with the black mane," she said to James, who was standing beside her. "On the race card, it says his name is Sultan's Pride. Which one do you think will win?"

James studied the horses through his binoculars. "I think the black one with the white star on his forehead," he said at last. "He looks really eager."

"That's Mr. Flash, I think," Mandy said, running her finger down the names on her race card. "What about you, Dad?" she asked as Dr. Adam came to stand next to her.

"Um. Let me see," began her dad, but he was too late because the horses suddenly surged away from the start. They swarmed over the first obstacle, an open ditch, in a fluid stream of heads and legs, then charged toward a series of ten hurdles.

Mandy gasped as two horses stumbled when they landed, falling to their knees and catapulting their jockeys into the air. But within seconds, the horses were back on their feet and cantering after the rest of the field with reins and stirrups flapping, while their riders walked off the track uninjured, brushing themselves off.

"Just shows how much the horses love racing," remarked Dr. Emily, watching them through her binoculars. "They keep going even when their riders fall off."

The horses raced up the hill and thundered down the home stretch, clearing the remaining fences with no further mishaps. With only seven hundred yards to go, a deafening roar rose from the grandstand as spectators yelled out the names of their favorite horses. The excitement reached fever pitch even inside the Sheldons' private box.

"Go, Sultan's Pride!" Mandy shouted as the gray horse took the lead.

But moments later, a black horse pulled ahead, its nose stretched forward and its ears back.

"It's Mr. Flash!" yelled James as his horse surged past the finish line to win by a short head.

James lifted his arms in triumph. "I won!"

"Congratulations." Mandy laughed. "Let's hope you can work the same magic for Bright Spark."

After the dessert, which was hot apple pie with ice cream, Mandy asked if she and James could go back to the stables to see Bright Spark once more before his race.

"Sure," said Mark. "I'll have to come with you, otherwise the race officials won't let you in." He put on his blazer, which he'd hung over the back of his chair, then said to Mandy's parents, "Seeing as you're officially Bright Spark's owners today, you might want to join me in the parade ring before the race."

"We'll be there," Dr. Adam promised.

Mark walked Mandy and James to the stable yard and left them at the entrance, saying he wanted to have a word with Gary in the changing rooms. Mandy led the way across the yard to Bright Spark's stall.

Unlike most of the horses in the row, Bright Spark wasn't looking out. Instead, his hindquarters were turned toward the door, and his head was deep in the shadows in the corner of the stall.

"That's odd," Mandy remarked, remembering how the racehorse had always looked out to greet them before.

"I expect Hayley's talking to him," suggested James as they pushed the door open and went inside.

"Hayley?" Mandy began. She could just see a figure standing at the horse's head, offering him an apple. She stopped abruptly when she realized that it wasn't Hayley. Then as the figure turned and looked at her, she exclaimed, "Phil! What are you doing here?"

# Seven

"I thought you weren't coming to the race," Mandy said.

Phil looked taken aback to see them in the stall. "I was just, er, just, um, giving Sparky a lucky apple," he stammered as the thoroughbred crunched noisily behind him.

"That's not a bad idea," James smiled. "I bet apples are his favorite. He really enjoyed the one I gave him the other day."

Phil didn't reply. Instead, he gave Bright Spark a quick pat on his shoulder and, without another word, brushed past Mandy and James and hurried out of the stall.

Mandy stared after him. "He's kind of odd, isn't he?" she whispered to James.

"Yeah. A bit of a dark, er, horse," said James, grinning.

Just then, Hayley came into the stable carrying a saddle and bridle. A red-and-gold cloth was folded on top of the saddle.

"Who's a dark horse?" asked Hayley, overhearing James.

"Phil," said Mandy. "He was here just now, wishing Bright Spark good luck. But he seemed a bit tense when we said hello."

Hayley rested the saddle on the door and laid the bridle on top of it. "Funny guy, Phil," she remarked. "He told me yesterday that he didn't think he wanted to watch the race. He certainly didn't come in the van with us. I guess he must have changed his mind and gotten a lift here with someone else." She took a wide-toothed plastic comb out of her pocket and gave it to Mandy. "Do you want to run that through Bright Spark's tail for me, please?"

"Sure," said Mandy. She started combing the horse's jet-black tail, making sure there were no tangles in it. It felt like silk in her fingers. "Maybe Phil's still worried about Bright Spark after he crashed at the fence the other day," she suggested.

"Yes. Perhaps he's scared that it'll happen again," James agreed.

"Could be," said Hayley. She unfolded the red-and-gold cloth on Bright Spark's back, then picked up the lightweight saddle from the door and gently placed it on top of the cloth. "It takes a while to get over an accident like that one, and we all know how fond Phil is of Sparky." She straightened the cloth under the saddle, then tightened the girth before slipping a bridle over Bright Spark's head. "Come on, boy," she said, gripping the rubber-covered reins in one hand. "Time to go."

Mandy felt a tingle run down her spine. The moment she'd been waiting for was here at last. The most beautiful horse at the track was about to make his appearance. And best of all, he was running on behalf of Animal Ark!

"Who's that?" asked James as he pushed open the door.

"Who's who?" said Hayley, leading Bright Spark out.

"That man — the one Phil's talking to," said James, pointing toward two men as he and Mandy followed Bright Spark into the yard.

Mandy looked where he was pointing. Near the parade ring, Phil was in deep conversation with a short, wiry man with thinning brown hair.

"Oh, that's Bob Fidler," said Hayley, "Phil's old boss and Bright Spark's former owner."

The two men were facing each other, Bob Fidler with his arms crossed and a determined expression on his face. Phil was gesturing angrily with his uninjured arm.

"It looks like they're arguing," Mandy remarked.

"Yeah, but that's typical of Bob Fidler," said Hayley. "He's famous for having a temper."

Mandy saw Phil shrug before turning and walking away. His former boss leaned against the railings and stared after him, then he straightened up and studied the horses that were entering the parade ring.

"Does Mr. Fidler have any horses in this race?" Mandy asked Hayley as they walked across the pavement with Bright Spark striding calmly beside them.

"Two, I think," Hayley told her. "But they're not his own. He's a trainer, like Mark, so he's responsible for other people's horses."

"I think he's coming over," whispered James as Mr. Fidler left the railing and walked toward them.

"I can't imagine why," muttered Hayley. "He hasn't been in touch with Mark about Bright Spark since he sold him."

But to Mandy's surprise, the trainer seemed very interested in the horse he'd once owned. "He's looking grand," he said, running his eyes appreciatively over the thoroughbred's glossy coat. "And I see he's the favorite to win."

Mandy was about to ask Mr. Fidler to point out his horses when she saw Mark and her mom and dad coming over. Gary was with them, too, wearing the Hare Hill colors, red and gold. He looked serious, but smiled when he saw Mandy and James.

Bob Fidler greeted them with a friendly wave. "Your horse is looking good," he said to Mark. "No doubt you're expecting him to do well."

"Absolutely," said Mark. "He's in top form."

"I heard he met a fence on the wrong side the other day," Bob remarked casually. "You don't think it might happen again?"

"No," said Mark confidently.

Mandy jumped to Bright Spark's defense. "It was just a freak accident. It could happen to any horse." She exchanged a glance with her dad, who nodded at her encouragingly. Then she reached up and smoothed Bright Spark's mane. The horse turned his head to blow softly in her hair.

"I daresay you're right about it being an accident, young lady," said Mr. Fidler. He seemed amused by Mandy's loyalty, because the corners of his mouth curled up in the faintest of smiles. "Anyway, I just came over to wish you all good luck." He shook Mark's hand. Lifting his cap to Dr. Emily, he strode into the parade ring.

Mark gave Bright Spark a firm pat on his shoulder. "Now, remember," he said to Gary. "Stay in the middle of the field until the last couple of lengths, then push for some extra acceleration up the hill to the homestretch."

"Got you," said Gary, and he followed Bright Spark and Hayley into the parade ring.

Mandy's parents and Mark went in, too. They stood in the center with Gary while Hayley walked Bright Spark around the ring with the other horses.

Mandy would have loved to go in, too, but it was pretty crowded in there already and she didn't want to get in the way, so she and James watched from the railing. *And anyway, Bright Spark is Dad's prize*, she reminded herself.

Leaning forward with her chin resting on her hands on the top railing, she looked closely at the horses being led around by their serious-faced stable hands. Most of the racehorses walked along quietly, but one or two pranced sideways, snorting loudly.

Mandy felt a ripple of pride when Hayley and Bright Spark went past her. "Go for it, Bright Spark," she called.

Hearing her, Hayley grinned over her shoulder and gave her a thumbs-up.

Grace Sheldon joined Mandy and James at the railing as a bell rang and the jockeys went over to their horses. "Just in time to wish them good luck," she said, waving to Gary. A strong gust of wind tugged at her hat. She held onto it to stop it from blowing away. "Mmm. I hope this doesn't mean rain," she said, glancing up grimly at the sky.

"Even if it does, I'm sure Bright Spark will be fine," Mandy decided.

"Yeah. He looks very calm and collected," said James as Gary put on his cap and racing goggles, then bent his knee so that Mark could give him a boost into the saddle. He glanced across to Mandy and James and gave them a confident wave before riding Bright Spark out of the ring.

"Quick. Let's watch them going down the straight to the start," said James. He ran toward the track, dodging through the crowds, who had obviously had the same idea, and Mandy ran after him.

"Go up to the box," called Mrs. Sheldon. "The view's better from there."

Mandy and James charged up the grandstand steps two at a time. They burst through the door and arrived on the balcony just as the horses were cantering past on their way to the start.

The loudspeaker crackled and the commentator began to introduce the horses. "And here's the favorite at two to one, number seven, Bright Spark, owned by Mark Sheldon and ridden by Gary Hart," he announced. There was a cheer from the crowd. Bright Spark was obviously very popular.

Feeling a surge of excitement welling up inside her, Mandy lifted her binoculars and focused them on Bright Spark. With his vibrant bay coat, striking white blaze, and long black legs, he stood out from the others like a shining beacon. "No wonder he's called Bright Spark," she said, keeping the binoculars firmly trained on the horse.

"He looks wonderful," remarked James. "You'd never think he'd had a bad fall the other day."

Not far from the starting tape, the racehorses disappeared for a few minutes behind a dense clump of trees. While the group was hidden, Mandy scanned the spectators in the grandstand.

"Hey! There's Phil," Mandy said, spotting the boy by the railing just in front of the finish line. He was easy to pick out, with one arm in a broad triangular sling. He certainly didn't look like the other cheerful, excited racegoers. Instead, he was pacing up and down, frowning deeply.

"He's a nervous wreck!" exclaimed James.

"I don't know why," said Mark, coming onto the balcony with his mother and Mandy's parents. "He knows Bright Spark has done well in training this week and the fall was just a freak accident."

"Yes, but he's really crazy about him," Mandy said sympathetically. "He probably can't help worrying, especially as someone else is riding him today."

"You might have a point there, Mandy," agreed Grace Sheldon. She pulled her coat more closely around her as the wind grew stronger and blew into the grandstand. "Brrr," she said, and shivered. "I'm going to watch from inside the box."

"Me, too," said Dr. Emily, going in with her and sliding the door shut.

The horses emerged from behind the trees. They had bunched together so that it was a few moments before Mandy picked out Bright Spark again. And when she did, her heart skipped a beat. The barely contained energy that he'd shown going past the grandstand had vanished. With his head down and ears back, he had slowed to a heavy, plodding walk.

"What's the matter with him?" Mandy asked, puzzled.

"What do you mean?" James raised his binoculars.

"Just look at him," said Mandy. "He's almost dragging his feet."

"What's Gary playing at?" muttered Mark, staring anxiously through his field glasses.

The racehorses reached the starting line and began to line up, jostling for position — except for Bright Spark, who stood miserably at the back, his flanks hunched up. Mandy could see Gary trying to coax him forward, but Bright Spark clearly didn't want to move. A steward went over to help, holding onto his hat as the wind tried to whip it away. He slipped one hand through Bright Spark's bridle, then led him to the line.

Mark looked very worried. "It doesn't make sense," he said. "He was all right five minutes ago."

Dr. Adam was equally concerned. "He's definitely not happy. I wonder if he's pulled a muscle?" He put down his binoculars. "I'd better have a look at him," he told Mark. "Can you pull him out of the race at this late stage?"

"I'll see if I can reach the race steward," replied Mark, taking his cell phone out of his jacket pocket.

The wind was picking up steadily. It whipped around Mandy, stinging her face. She turned her head to one side to avoid the damp, icy blast. And as she did, it suddenly dawned on her why Bright Spark was behaving so strangely. "Hang on!" she cried. She pointed up at the sky. Heavy black clouds had gathered, and the air was laden with moisture.

"It's going to rain," she announced. "That's why Bright Spark's acting up. He hasn't gotten over his rain phobia after all!"

# *Eight*

As soon as Mandy had spoken, the heavens opened and gray bullets of rain pelted down onto the racecourse. At the same time, the starter lifted the tape and the horses sprang forward, with Bright Spark setting off a good stride behind the others.

"Go, Bright Spark!" Mandy yelled, even though she knew he couldn't hear her.

James cupped his hands around his mouth. "It's only rain. It won't hurt you," he shouted.

Through her binoculars, Mandy could see Gary leaning forward in the saddle, crouched over the black mane. But she realized with a feeling of dread that all the encouragement in the world wasn't going to make any difference. Bright Spark was already trailing at the back of the field, looking thoroughly miserable.

"Come on, Bright Spark," shouted Dr. Adam. "You can do it."

"Blast this rain!" exclaimed Mark as the other nine horses opened up the gap.

A black horse at the back of the field refused to jump the first fence. Bright Spark was a few heads behind, and Mandy half expected him to refuse the fence, too. She breathed a sigh of relief when Gary managed to get him over. But Bright Spark was barely going faster than a canter in spite of Gary's efforts.

Mandy rolled her hands into tight fists. "Come on, Bright Spark!" she shouted. But with the other horses powering their way up the hill, she knew in her heart that her dad's prize horse had already lost the race. It was agonizing to watch the beautiful bay thoroughbred as he blundered his way over the hurdles in painful slow motion, often clipping the tops with his hooves and stumbling heavily when he landed.

Ahead of him, the other racehorses galloped smoothly up the homestretch. The cries of encouragement from the crowd gradually faded and were replaced by a stunned silence as everyone realized that the race favorite was nowhere to be seen.

A big gray horse took the lead about a thousand yards from the finish. There were a few muted cheers from spectators as he thundered past the winning post two lengths ahead of the rest of the field and far ahead of the jockey wearing the scarlet-and-gold colors.

"That should have been Bright Spark," James blurted out, disappointment written all over his face.

"It would have been if it hadn't rained," Mandy said, watching Bright Spark trail across the finish line with rain falling in sheets around him.

"We've got a lot of work to do with that horse," muttered Mark. Below them, Bright Spark had pulled up, his head dropping and his sides heaving. Gary sat hunched in the saddle and stared at the ground, holding the reins loosely in one hand.

Mark was clearly very upset. "Sorry your prize turned out to be such a dud, Adam," he said.

"Don't worry. It's just one of those things," Mandy's dad reassured him.

Dr. Emily and Grace Sheldon came out onto the balcony. "How utterly disappointing," said Mrs. Sheldon. "Bright Spark looked so good going down to the start."

"There was no hint that anything was wrong before the race," said Dr. Emily, running one hand through her shoulder-length red hair. "It was like watching a different horse."

"In all the years I've owned horses, I've never known one to be so upset by rain," said Mrs. Sheldon.

Mark shook his head in disbelief. "Pity I didn't know how bad he was before I bought him," he murmured.

"Didn't Phil say anything?" Mandy asked. She could see the boy down at the railings. He was walking away from the track looking as gloomy as ever. "I mean, he must know Bright Spark better than anyone."

"He didn't say much," Mark admitted. "Just that Sparky could be a bit nervous in the rain. But this was more than a bit nervous!" He put down his binoculars and went toward the door. "I'm going down to have a word with Gary. Anyone want to join me?"

"We should really have a look at Bright Spark," suggested Dr. Emily. "Just in case there's something we can do to help."

Dr. Adam frowned. "I'm not sure there's a lot we can do to stop him from hating the rain."

On the way down the stairs, Mandy overheard snatches of conversation as people discussed Bright Spark's poor performance. "I'd heard such good things about that horse," grumbled one woman. "Who'd have thought he'd be last?"

Feeling stung, Mandy nearly jumped to Bright Spark's defense again, but she didn't want to appear rude. "He couldn't help it," she muttered under her breath. "Some horses just hate the rain."

They passed the winner's circle on the way to the collecting ring. Mandy saw the gray horse standing in the separate fenced-off area. His owner and rider were standing beside him. They looked very proud as a local council person presented them with a silver trophy.

"Look, there's Mr. Fidler," said James. Bright Spark's former owner was standing next to a dark brown horse in the area reserved for the runner-up. "That must be one of the horses he trained," James added.

They reached the ring to find Hayley already there. Gary had dismounted to let her throw a blanket over Bright Spark's hindquarters before leading him back to the stable.

Mandy went over and stroked Bright Spark's neck. "Poor boy," she said soothingly. "It wasn't your day, was it? But you can relax now. It looks like the rain's going to stop." Overhead, the clouds were thinning, and a pale yellow sun was trying to break through.

"He'll be all right once he's warm and dry," said Hayley.

As they trooped back to the stable yard, Mandy heard Gary telling Mark what had happened out on the track. "I just couldn't believe it," said the jockey. "I mean, he was fine leaving the parade ring, but as soon as we got out on the track he seemed to go to sleep. There was nothing I could do to wake him up."

Mark frowned and shook his head.

Inside the stable, Mandy and James helped Hayley remove the saddle and bridle, then they rubbed the horse down until he was almost dry. Next they buckled a thick blanket over him.

"You can cheer up now," said James, patting Bright Spark's shoulder.

But Bright Spark didn't even look at him. He stared forlornly at the wall in front of him.

"Be back in a minute," said Hayley, picking up the saddle and going out of the stall. "I'm just going to put the tack in the van."

Outside, Mandy's parents and Mark and his mother were still discussing the race with Gary. After awhile, Mandy became aware of another voice, and when she looked out the door, she saw that Bob Fidler had come over to join them. "Pity about Sparky's performance," he said.

"Yes. We're all rather shattered," Mrs. Sheldon responded.

"You never told me he was that bad in the rain," said Mark, his tone mild.

"He wasn't." Bob shrugged. "Maybe his fall the other day upset him."

"Seems rather unlikely to me," commented Dr. Emily.

"You never know," said Bob. He stood with his feet apart and his arms crossed in front of him. "And if you want my opinion, it's probably not worth trying him out again. Let's face it, if he hates the rain so much that he won't run in it, he'll never be any good on the track." He put a hand on Mark's shoulder. "I tell you what. I'll buy him back from you — not at the full price, of course, but he can live in my yard as a companion to my other steeplechasers. And when it rains," he added with a grin, "we'll make sure he's tucked up safely indoors."

Mandy could hardly bear to listen. Even if Mr. Fidler was trying to be helpful, it seemed horribly unfair to Bright Spark. She turned away and stroked the horse's sleek neck. To her relief, she heard Mark say, "Thanks, but no thanks, Bob. I won't give up on Bright Spark just yet. We'll deal with the rain problem somehow."

"Good!" whispered James, clearly sharing Mandy's feelings.

Mandy put her face close to Bright Spark's head. "Come on. You can't still be moping about that down-pour. It was over ages ago," she told the horse. But even as she spoke, she realized just how odd it was that Bright Spark was still looking so miserable. After all, it wasn't raining in here! And before he'd responded to her voice and touch, but now he didn't even seem to notice that she was there. In fact, the horse looked even worse than when he'd just finished the race. His head was hanging limply and his eyes were half closed.

An uneasy feeling crept over Mandy. She shot James a worried look. "I don't think he's well," she said.

James frowned. "He was fine earlier," he reminded her. He reached into his pocket and brought out an apple. "Look, I brought this from home as a treat for him. Let's see if it helps." He offered it to Bright Spark, but the racehorse didn't even sniff it.

"That's it," said Mandy. "He's definitely not well." She spun around and hurried outside to her dad. "I'm sure something's wrong with Bright Spark," she said quietly to him. "I don't think it was the rain that upset him after all."

"What makes you think that?" asked Dr. Adam.

"Well, he's not reacting to us like he used to," Mandy said. "It's like he's in a trance."

Dr. Adam looked thoughtful. "After the way you picked up on Pandora's symptoms, I guess you know a sick animal when you see one," he said. "So let's check him out."

Mark had overheard their hushed conversation. "You mean there could be more to his symptoms than not liking the rain?" he asked anxiously.

"That's what I'm going to find out," answered Dr. Adam. "But I'm going to need some instruments to examine him thoroughly."

"You mean like stethoscopes and things?" said Gary.

"That's right," Dr. Adam replied.

"I'll get some from the racehorse vet," offered Gary, and he brushed past Bob, then ran across the yard to the vet's office at the end of the stable block.

While they were waiting for Gary to return, Dr. Emily and Dr. Adam went into the stable and felt Bright Spark's legs to see if a muscle stain could be troubling him.

"I hope it's nothing serious," said Mrs. Sheldon, standing in the doorway with Mark. She held her well-manicured hands to her face as she watched Mandy's mom and dad move quietly around the horse.

Dr. Emily stood up after running her hand down the horse's legs. "Nothing wrong there," she said. "No heat, no swelling, no signs of any knocks."

Gary appeared with the racecourse vet's bag. Dr. Adam took out the stethoscope and listened to Bright Spark's heart and breathing. "That's all fine," he said, then he shone a flashlight into the horse's eyes.

Standing close by, Mandy could see that Bright Spark's eyes looked glazed over, the pupils huge and unmoving. "It's like he has a concussion," she said, wonderingly.

"Yes. Sort of spaced out, like Phil was after his fall," James remembered.

Dr. Adam put the instruments away and snapped the bag shut. Dr. Emily stood back, looking quizzically at the horse. She exchanged a knowing look with her husband. "Are you thinking what I'm thinking?" she murmured.

Mandy's heart raced as she waited for her parents' diagnosis. She crossed her fingers in her coat pockets and saw that James was doing the same.

"I think so," Dr. Adam answered. He looked at Mark.

"There's nothing physically wrong with Bright Spark," he announced. "Not in terms of an infection or virus, at least."

"So it *was* the rain that made him like this," stated Mrs. Sheldon.

"No. The rain had nothing to do with it. In fact, I'd say he probably didn't even notice it," said Dr. Adam. He passed a hand in front of Bright Spark's eyes. The horse didn't blink.

"He's like a zombie," said James.

"That just about sums it up," agreed Dr. Adam. "And there can be only one explanation."

"What's that?" Mandy blurted out.

Dr. Adam put a hand on Mark's shoulder and looked very grave. "I'm afraid Bright Spark's been drugged."

## *Nine*

Drugged! Mandy could hardly believe her ears. "Who would have drugged him? And why?" She gasped. But her disbelief quickly faded as Bright Spark's sudden loss of form, his glazed expression, and his drooping head began to make awful sense to her. "No wonder you don't even recognize us," she said, gently stroking the horse's nose.

Mark was ashen-faced. "It's impossible," he said, while next to him, his mother shook her head.

"What's impossible?" asked Hayley, returning to the stable with a bucket of water. "What's going on?"

"Bright Spark's been drugged," James told her.

Hayley stopped abruptly in the doorway. "Oh, my goodness! I should have guessed."

"There was no reason to," Mrs. Sheldon said. "Nothing like this has ever happened to us before."

Outside, Bob Fidler was craning his neck to see what was going on. He caught Mandy's eye, then hurriedly put on his cap and slipped away as a voice came over the loudspeaker to announce the start of the next race.

"Are you absolutely sure about this?" Mark persisted, coming into the stall.

Dr. Adam nodded. "As sure as I can be without doing a blood test."

"Then I want one taken," decided Mark. "We'll be disqualified from the race if the test is positive, but that's irrelevant when the horse's health is at risk. I need to know exactly what's going on here."

"OK," said Dr. Adam. "It would be helpful to know what drug was used, because there might be an antidote for it. But even if there isn't, I'm sure Bright Spark will be fine in a while." He opened the vet's bag and took out a swab and a bottle of surgical alcohol.

There was a hushed silence as Dr. Adam soaked the swab, then wiped it over Bright Spark's neck. A movement outside caught Mandy's attention, and she saw Phil standing behind Hayley and Mrs. Sheldon. There was a look of terror on his face as he peered into the stall and saw Dr. Adam preparing to take a blood sample from the horse.

"It's OK, Phil," said Mandy, going over to the door. "Bright Spark's not ill. Dad thinks he's been drugged. But he should be OK when the drugs are out of his system."

Phil opened his mouth to talk but closed it again without saying anything.

Mark went out of the stall and rested a sympathetic hand on the boy's shoulder. "Perhaps you should go and see if you can cheer Bright Spark up."

Phil stared at the horse, then looked back at Mark. "I, er," he stammered before falling silent once more. Then he shuffled into the stall and stood next to Dr. Adam, who was taking a needle and syringe out of the vet's bag.

The stable boy's reaction puzzled Mandy. Phil adored the horse, yet it was as if he didn't want to be with him right now. Perhaps he just couldn't stand to see Bright Spark looking so strange.

Outside, Mark ran his hands through his blond hair in frustration. "I don't know who could have done it," he said. "Or when, for that matter. I mean, Hayley was with him all the time — from when they left Hare Hill until Gary mounted him in the parade ring. Isn't that right, Hayley?"

Hayley nodded. "Yes, except for a few seconds when I went to get the tack."

"And that's when we arrived, wasn't it?" James said to Mandy.

"And even then, Bright Spark wasn't alone," Mandy added. She turned to Phil. "You were with him, weren't . . ." Her voice trailed away as a terrible suspicion flooded her mind.

The boy looked at her, his face stricken, and nodded. Then he stepped forward and put his hand on Dr. Adam's arm. "Don't," he said, just as Dr. Adam was about to insert the needle. "You don't have to test his blood. Bright Spark has definitely been doped, and I can tell you what the drug is."

It was as if a bolt of lightening suddenly struck the crowded stable. "What?" cried Dr. Emily.

Mark stared in horror at Phil. He took a step forward, his face blazing with anger. "How dare you?"

Phil dropped his head. "I'm so sorry," he muttered. "I should never have let myself get caught up in it."

"Caught up in what?" Mark shot back angrily.

"In trying to make Bright Spark look hopeless," replied Phil. He put his uninjured arm over Bright Spark's neck and hugged him. "I'm sorry to have done this to you, boy. It was downright stupid of me."

"More than stupid. It was criminal," Mark warned. "What did you give him?"

"A couple of tranquilizers," answered Phil. "I hid them in — "

"The apple!" James broke in. "So it wasn't a lucky apple after all."

"No. More like a *laced* apple," said Mark, through clenched teeth.

Dr. Adam was putting the syringe back in the bag. "At least we know what we're dealing with now," he said. "And there's not much we can do other than let Bright Spark rest. He'll feel dopey for a while, but he'll soon be over it."

Mark still looked thunderstruck. "Why on earth did you do it?" he asked Phil, going into the stall. "For money? Are you in some kind of trouble?"

Mandy bit a thumbnail as she waited for Phil's response. He had seemed so devoted to Bright Spark. Could he really have been bribed to drug the horse he loved so much?

Phil stroked Bright Spark's rain-damp mane. "It wasn't for money," he said quietly. "It was because I want to be a jockey."

"But you *were* going to be Bright Spark's jockey. When you were ready," Mrs. Sheldon pointed out. "How on earth was doping him going to help?"

Phil pushed back his cap and stared out the stall door. "I've always wanted to be a lead jockey. And when Bob Fidler offered to make me his lead jockey if I slipped Sparky some tranquilizers, I stupidly jumped at the chance."

Mandy shot James a look of surprise. Mr. Fidler had been so impressed with Bright Spark before the race. In a way, he'd seemed almost envious. So that's what it was all about. "Of course!" Mandy declared. "Mr. Fidler knew his horses didn't stand a chance against Bright Spark."

"And that's why he wanted him out of the way," finished James, thinking along the same lines as Mandy.

"No. It was nothing like that," Phil told them. "It's because Mr. Fidler wants to buy Bright Spark back. He figured that if the horse did badly, he'd get him back at a really low price."

"But that's cheating!" Mandy said, and gasped.

"It certainly is," agreed Mark. "What's more, Fidler was badly mistaken. And he knows that." He glared at Phil over the horse's back. "I can't believe you went along with it."

Phil rested his head against Bright Spark's neck. "I know," he murmured sadly. "It seemed like a good plan at first, but the more I thought about it, the more I realized I didn't want to be mixed up in it."

"So why didn't you just say no?" Mandy asked.

"I tried to. But Mr. Fidler wouldn't let me back out of the deal. He threatened to tell the race officials that I was planning to drug a horse."

James pushed his glasses up his nose. "You could have denied it."

"It would have been his word against mine." Phil shrugged.

Mandy was appalled at what Phil had done, but there was a small part of her that felt sorry for him. He seemed genuinely remorseful for what he'd done, and there was no denying that he loved Bright Spark. "At least you realized you were doing the wrong thing," she said.

"Yeah. I hated myself for agreeing to drug Sparky. I reckon I must have been out of my mind at the time. So that's why I came up with my own plan," admitted Phil.

"You mean there's more?" demanded Mark. "What else have you done to my horse?"

Phil looked very uncomfortable. He stroked Bright Spark's neck. Then, taking a deep breath, he dropped the next bombshell. "It was my fault that Bright Spark fell up at the run the other day," he explained, looking squarely into Mark's eyes. "I deliberately got the stride wrong at the hurdle in the hope that you would decide not to race him today. I wouldn't have had to drug him then, you see."

Phil's confession was met with a stunned silence that was broken when Mark said angrily, "I can't believe what I'm hearing. You dared to put my horse, and even yourself, at risk just because of a stupid decision you'd made?"

"I was desperate," murmured Phil. "I had to do something. But the plan backfired."

"Yes, with you just about killing yourself," blurted out James.

"Better me than Sparky," said Phil sincerely. "I'd never have forgiven myself if you'd been injured," he whispered to the horse.

"Well, here's something else you won't be able to forgive yourself for," announced Mark. "You're fired. Immediately." He went over to the door and stood to one side. "I want you to leave right away," he ordered.

"But I was only — " stammered the boy.

"I've heard enough," Mark interrupted him. "Nothing you can say will make me change my mind. I will not have my staff tampering with the horses. Go now, or you'll have to answer to the race officials."

Mandy saw Phil swallow hard before wrapping his arms around Bright Spark's neck and hugging him again. "It looks like it's the end of the road for us, boy," he whispered.

Bright Spark blinked and lifted his head slightly. It was his first response to anything since he'd come off the track. For a brief, hopeful moment, Mandy thought he was coming around, but then he dropped his head again.

"I'll miss you," continued Phil.

Mark was still at the door, waiting for Phil to leave. "Come on. You're just dragging it out," he said impatiently.

"Won't you give me another chance?" implored Phil, looking back over his shoulder at Mark. "I promise I'll never let you down again."

Mark shook his head in stony silence.

Mandy felt another wave of sympathy for Phil. He'd made a bad mistake, but at least he'd owned up to what he'd done. But coming clean had cost him his job, and even worse, the horse he loved so dearly. Mandy caught James's eye and realized that he, too, felt sorry for the stable boy. If only there were something they could do to help him.

Phil gave Bright Spark a sad look, then turned and went toward the door. Bright Spark blinked again and lifted his head to watch his boy walk away.

Feeling desperate for both Phil and Bright Spark,

Mandy appealed to her mom and dad. "You've got to help Phil," she said quietly. "He hasn't really harmed Bright Spark. And he's so devoted to him."

"But what can we do?" asked Dr. Adam.

"I don't know. Put in a good word for him?" Mandy suggested, not at all sure that her dad would agree. After all, he was a vet, which meant he would take a very dim view of people who drugged animals.

Suddenly, Dr. Emily said to Mark, "You know that no permanent harm's been done to Bright Spark, don't you?"

Mark looked at her, his eyebrows raised.

"There'll only be one side effect after today," Mandy's mom continued. "And it's something a vet can't do anything about."

"What's that?" asked Mark, a new note of concern in his voice.

"Heartache," said Dr. Emily bluntly. "That horse will miss Phil a lot. There's a strong bond between them, you can't deny that."

"That's not reason enough to keep Phil on," said Mark, watching the stable boy walking slowly across the yard with his head down.

"Oh, but it is," Mandy blurted out. "Bright Spark was definitely beginning to respond to Phil just now."

"And now he's totally miserable again," James added.

The racehorse was staring after Phil. His eyes were still glazed, but there was a sadness in them, as if he knew he'd never see his stable boy again.

"Phil's not the only one who can take care of him," said Mark. "Hayley's quite capable, aren't you?"

Hayley looked embarrassed. "I guess," she muttered. "But those two were really close."

Mrs. Sheldon put a hand on Mark's arm. "Probably as close as you and Knight's Dance were once."

Mandy noticed Mark's expression soften. Silently, she willed him to change his mind. And then, as if the memory of the famous horse had triggered something in him, Mark said, "I guess Phil did save us from having to go on a wild goose chase to find out who was behind the drugging."

"If he'd kept quiet, we might never have found out the truth," Dr. Adam agreed.

"And Bob Fidler might even have found another way to get Bright Spark back," remarked Mrs. Sheldon.

"I don't know about that," said Mark. "Still, I guess Phil deserves some credit for telling us everything."

Mandy held her breath.

The trainer rested his chin in one hand and looked thoughtful. Then he pushed his way out of the stall and ran after the boy. "Phil!" he called, beckoning to him. "I need a word with you."

"Let's hope it's a good word," James whispered to Mandy.

Phil stopped. He hesitated before slowly retracing his footsteps, his face creased with worry. Mandy wondered what was going through his head. Perhaps he thought Mark had decided to call the stewards and make a formal charge.

"I've had second thoughts," said Mark when Phil stopped in front of him.

Phil looked more worried than ever.

"You can stay," said Mark, "but on one condition."

"Anything you say," promised the relieved stable boy.

"While you're working at Hare Hill, you may not have any contact with Bob Fidler," said Mark. "If you do, I'll report you both to the racing commission. And I'm sure Adam and Emily would provide a statement if necessary." He glanced across at Mandy's parents, who nodded gravely.

Phil didn't hesitate. "I'll stay totally clear of him. And this time you can trust me a hundred percent. I've learned my lesson."

"I sincerely hope so," said Mark. "And there's one more thing. You won't be riding in any races until I judge you to be well and truly ready. You're going to have to convince me that you won't be making any more mistakes like the one at the hurdle."

Mandy expected Phil to be disappointed by this. But if he was, he didn't show it. Instead, he went straight over to Bright Spark and stroked his forelock. "It's all my fault that you're feeling like this. But I'm going to stay with you until you're back to normal." He turned to Dr. Emily and Dr. Adam. "Is there anything I should be doing to help him?"

"Not really," answered Dr. Adam. "Other than keeping an eye on him and making sure he's warm and has food and water if he wants it."

"Then that's what I'll do," said Phil. He hurried out of the stall and returned moments later with a bulging hay net and a blanket that was even bigger and thicker than the one Bright Spark was already wearing.

Mark seemed satisfied with Phil's promise, so when Mrs. Sheldon suggested they all go back to the box for tea, he agreed.

Hayley left, too, saying she had to start preparing Jackdaw's Lad for his big race.

"Would you like us to stay and help you?" Mandy asked Phil as the others walked away.

"Sure, thanks," said Phil, stripping off Bright Spark's blanket to replace it with the thicker one.

Mandy helped Phil drape the blanket over the horse while James folded up the other blanket and hung it over the door.

"Thanks for sticking up for me, you guys," said Phil, fiddling with a piece of straw in his fingers. "I heard what you said to Mr. Sheldon."

"Well, I could tell you were really sorry for what you'd done," Mandy said.

"Yeah! It was so dumb," said Phil, angry at himself. "And thanks to me, Sparky's like this."

"He'll recover soon enough," said James. "Won't he, Mandy?"

"Oh, yes," she replied, remembering what her mom

had said a few minutes before. But she could see Phil wasn't convinced, and Mandy was finding it hard to stay positive herself. Bright Spark still seemed so limp, almost lifeless even. He stared blankly at the ground, his head drooping as if he didn't have the strength to hold it up. How long would it take for the drugs to wear off?

# *Ten*

"You'd think he'd be coming out of it by now," Mandy said to Phil.

"I never thought the drugs would affect him like this," Phil muttered. "Bob Fidler said they would just slow him down." He clenched his fist and slammed it into the palm of the hand in the sling, apparently forgetting for a moment that his wrist was broken. He winced and sucked in his breath.

"You shouldn't keep blaming yourself," Mandy told him. "And it's not as if you haven't paid for what you did, what with knocking yourself out, breaking your wrist, and nearly losing your job."

"As well as nearly turning into a nervous wreck over the whole thing," added James. He took out the apple he'd offered Bright Spark earlier and tried to tempt him with it again. But even though James held it right under his nose, the horse ignored it.

"I suppose we'll just have to be patient and wait until the drugs have gone through his system," Mandy said. She looked out over the stall door. The horses for the seventh race were leaving the parade ring on their way to the starting line. This meant there was only one race left to go. After everything that had happened, Mandy had almost forgotten that Mark had another horse to run. She felt a flutter of excitement in the pit of her stomach. "It's all up to Jackdaw's Lad now," she said to James.

"He'll be terrific," James replied confidently.

"I hope so," said Mandy. The main race had attracted some of the best steeplechase horses in the county, and Jackdaw's Lad was going to be up against some very stiff competition.

A clatter of hooves sounded from the stall next door. Mandy turned and saw Hayley leading Jackdaw's Lad into the yard. "Wow!" she whispered. The chestnut gelding looked magnificent. His coat gleamed in the fading winter sun, and he held his head high as he walked proudly across the cobbles.

"You must have been grooming him for ages," Mandy said when Hayley stopped in front of her.

"To tell the truth, I have," Hayley confessed with a smile. "After what happened with Bright Spark, I want everyone to sit up and take notice of Jackdaw's Lad." She gave the horse a pat on his shoulder. "You're going to show them just how good the Hare Hill team really is, aren't you, boy?"

Jackdaw's Lad tossed his head and snorted.

"I'll take that to mean yes," said Hayley. She squinted over the stall door at Bright Spark. "How's he doing?"

James appeared in the doorway. "Much the same, really," he said, wrinkling his nose. "He's still very quiet."

A loudspeaker in the yard crackled to life. "The seventh race is about to start," came the commentator's nasal voice. "They're at the start," he said. Then, after a brief pause, he called out, "And they're off!"

The commentator's volley of words tumbled out at a speed that matched the horses' pace as they hurtled up the track and over the hurdles toward the finish line.

Mandy's stomach churned. Very soon, Jackdaw's Lad would be racing over the same hurdles.

Hayley gave the lead rein a gentle tug. "Right, boy. Let's take you to Gary in the parade ring," she said. "Are you coming to cheer him on?" she asked.

"Definitely," Mandy answered. She glanced back at

Phil, who was sitting in the straw with his back against the stall wall. "You don't mind if James and I desert you for a while, do you?"

"No. Go and enjoy the race," said Phil. "I'll keep an eye on Sparky." He reached up and caught the apple that James tossed to him.

"That's for Bright Spark. In case he comes round and is ravenous," James told him.

On the way to the parade ring, Jackdaw's Lad grew more and more restless. He thrashed his head up and down, then reared up on his hind legs.

"Here we go again," said James grimly, dodging out of the way.

"Easy, easy," soothed Hayley, holding the lead rein firmly in both hands.

Jackdaw's Lad jerked his head up, nearly pulling the rein out of Hayley's hands.

"No, you don't," said Hayley. She stopped and steadied him, then continued toward the ring.

"Gary's going to have his hands full if he keeps this up," remarked James. He glanced across to the middle of the parade ring where Mark and Mrs. Sheldon were standing with the jockey, frowning worriedly at Jackdaw's Lad. Mandy's parents were also watching the horse, but they were on the far side of the parade ring, close to the grandstand.

"Well, he's not going to keep it up," Hayley said firmly. She looked around quickly, as if to make sure no one was listening, then in a low voice said, "Could you two do something really important for me, please?"

"We'll try," said James.

"What is it?" Mandy asked.

"Do you think you could get Parsley from the van and smuggle him over here?" said Hayley.

"That's a great idea," Mandy said. "She'll calm Jack down."

"Just don't let anyone else see her. We don't want her upsetting the other horses," Hayley called after them as they hurried away.

Parsley was curled up on the plaid blanket on the passenger's seat in the cab of the Hare Hill van. Her head shot up as soon as James opened the door, and when she saw who it was, she leaped to her feet and wagged her long, thin tail.

"We have a very important job for you to do," Mandy told the little dog, picking Parsley up and tucking her into her jacket.

"We might need this," said James, pocketing a leash he'd found on the dashboard.

With Parsley well hidden, Mandy and James ran back to the parade ring. They arrived just as Gary was walking across to mount Jackdaw's Lad. The wild expression in the gelding's eyes was enough to tell Mandy that he was even more keyed up than before.

"Quick," said James. "Let's go over to that tree." There was an old oak growing next to the railing, just a few yards from where Jackdaw's Lad was standing. "We can hide behind it so that no one sees Parsley." He waved to Hayley to get her attention, then followed Mandy behind the tree.

They peered out as Hayley whispered to Gary, then turned Jackdaw's Lad to face the railing.

"Say hello to your friend," Mandy said. She took Parsley out and put her on the ground. James quickly clipped the leash to her collar to stop her from running into the parade ring.

Parsley spotted her friend at once. She stood up on her hind legs and scratched against the fence post with her front paws.

"Just don't start barking again," Mandy murmured, remembering the huge fuss Parsley had made when she was nearly left behind at the stables the other day.

A bell rang and the jockeys began to mount their horses.

"Oh, no!" exclaimed James as Hayley gave Gary a leg up. "We're too late. Jack hasn't seen Parsley."

Gary heaved himself into the saddle, and Jackdaw's Lad wheeled around, his tail streaming out like a silky orange kite. Suddenly, he stood perfectly still. He sniffed the air, turned his head, and stared straight at Parsley, his ears flicked forward and his nostrils flared. To Mandy's delight, the nervous glint in the horse's eyes vanished and he started to breathe more evenly.

"Phew!" Mandy sighed. "Just in time." She picked up Parsley and tucked the terrier inside her jacket again. "Aren't you amazing?" she chuckled.

Hayley was beckoning to them from the entrance to the parade ring. The horses were filing past her on their way to the racetrack. Mandy and James hurried over to her. Mark and Mrs. Sheldon had left the ring on the far side and were heading for the grandstand with Mandy's mom and dad.

"That was perfect timing," said Hayley when Mandy and James reached her. Parsley peeped out from Mandy's jacket and Hayley patted the little dog on the top of her head. "Now for your next important job," she said.

"What's that?" Mandy asked.

"She's going to cheer Jackdaw's Lad down the home-stretch." Hayley grinned as she looped the lead rein over her shoulder. "Come on," she said.

They found a spot next to the railing and close to the finish line. They were just in time, because the crowd quickly swelled as more and more spectators arrived to cheer on the horses.

A heavy man in a tweed jacket and flat cap pushed his way to the front. He stood next to Mandy and peered through his binoculars at the twelve horses trotting up the track. "There's the winner," he muttered, just loud enough for Mandy to hear.

"You must be talking about Jackdaw's Lad," Mandy couldn't resist saying.

"No!" declared the man, still concentrating on the horses. "Thunderbolt's the one to watch for. The black gelding on the outside." He lowered his glasses and looked over the top of them at Mandy. "With him in the race, Jackdaw's Lad stands no chance."

"Of course he does," James said hotly. "You'll see."

The man looked at James with an amused expression. "You got inside information, kid?"

"Better than that," James told him. "We know Jackdaw's Lad personally. In fact, Hayley here is in charge of him. She'll tell you just how good he is."

"In that case, I'll take your word for it," joked the man as the commentator announced that the race was about to begin.

Mandy felt her stomach tie itself in knots. She lifted her binoculars and studied the horses lining up at the start. She quickly spotted the black one, Thunderbolt. He was stamping the ground impatiently. Jackdaw's Lad was three horses away from him.

The starter raised his arm, held it in the air for a moment, then dropped it. The starting tape flew up and the horses burst forward.

"Go, Jackdaw's Lad!" yelled James, his voice almost lost in the roar that erupted from the crowd.

Parsley squirmed madly inside Mandy's jacket. "OK, OK," Mandy said, lowering her binoculars and taking Parsley out so that she could see the horses.

It wasn't easy to hold a wriggling Jack Russell terrier that was yapping at the top of its voice. Mandy had to hold the little dog tightly in both hands, wrapping the leash several times around her wrist just in case Parsley managed to get away and go hurtling onto the track. But it was much more exciting to watch the race from the railing than up in the box.

Unable to hold up her binoculars, Mandy had to rely on her bare eyes. At the first hurdle, a rider came off his horse, which stumbled briefly before galloping after the others, leaving his jockey sitting dazed on the grass.

The horses thundered on. Bunched tightly together, they came to an open ditch and swarmed over it with hardly a break in the rhythm of the hooves on the turf.

"They're neck and neck!" shouted James, sounding just like the commentator. "It's anyone's race."

But at the sixth hurdle, a gray next to Jackdaw's Lad refused and swerved sideways, unseating his jockey.

For an agonizing moment, Mandy thought this would unsettle Jackdaw's Lad. But the only one who seemed upset was the fallen jockey, who punched the grass angrily, then watched in disappointment as his riderless horse stormed down the track after the others.

It was only when they reached the uphill stretch that the horses started to spread out. Thunderbolt quickly seized the lead, his jockey pushing him with every stride to open up the gap. Several lengths behind them came three other horses racing shoulder to shoulder, and next, in fifth place, was Jackdaw's Lad.

Mandy's heart pounded as she watched the chestnut surging up the hill. He seemed to be gaining on the group of three horses, but he was still several lengths behind the leader. "You can do it!" Mandy screamed at the top of her voice. In her arms, Parsley began yapping loudly as she caught sight of her friend.

"Go!" yelled Hayley, jumping up and down, while next to her James climbed onto the railing and waved his hands in the air.

"Come on, Jackdaw's Lad!" he roared.

The horses crested the top of the hill and galloped down the homestretch. Mandy could see Gary urging Jackdaw's Lad to go faster, kicking his heels against the gelding's sweat-streaked flanks. The chestnut responded by lengthening his stride, but even though he soon streaked past the three horses in front of him, he was still well behind Thunderbolt.

Parsley's shrill bark grew louder and more urgent as she saw her friend galloping toward her. But Mandy was sure Jackdaw's Lad would never hear the excited yapping above the din the crowd was making. With only five hundred yards to go and Thunderbolt still well in front, it looked as if nothing could help the chestnut win the race.

The stout man punched the air as his horse charged toward the finish line. But when Mandy glanced at the man's flushed face, she saw his expression change. She looked back at the horses and saw that Jackdaw's Lad and Thunderbolt were racing neck and neck.

Mandy clenched her fists. "You can do it," she screamed, and at the same time Parsley escaped from her arms and jumped down to the ground. Luckily, the leash was still wrapped around Mandy's wrist. She grabbed it with her other hand, but Parsley wasn't going anywhere. Like a seasoned racegoer, the terrier stood next to the railing and cheered her horse on.

Chestnut and black raced side by side toward the finish line. "It's going to be a tie!" shouted James, but he'd barely said the words when Jackdaw's Lad surged past Thunderbolt and crossed the line a hairbreadth in front of his opponent.

The roar that erupted from the crowd sounded like an earthquake. But Jackdaw's Lad didn't seem to hear. He dropped abruptly to a walk, his attention on one thing only — the railing where Parsley stood, her tail wagging in a blur of excitement. With Gary sitting in the saddle grinning from ear to ear, Jackdaw's Lad walked over to his friend and lowered his head to blow softly down his nostrils at the little dog.

Mandy stared in amazement. Was it really because of Parsley that Jackdaw's Lad had found the final burst of speed? "What a race!" she said to Gary.

His goggles spattered with mud, the jockey grinned broadly down at her. "I knew he could do it."

"You wonderful, wonderful, smart horse," enthused Hayley, ducking under the railing and throwing her arms around the chestnut's neck.

The heavy man shook his head in disbelief. He looked at James and smiled wryly. "I should have listened to you!" he said.

It was a jubilant group that gathered in the winner's circle ten minutes later. The Hopes and James stood next to Hayley and Gary and clapped enthusiastically as Mrs. Sheldon and Mark went up to receive the trophy, a big silver cup engraved with the names of the previous winners, several of which had gone on to become very famous indeed.

"Congratulations!" called Dr. Adam as Mark, beaming from ear to ear, turned and triumphantly held the trophy in the air.

"Thanks." Mark smiled. "And thanks for all your support."

"Don't mention it," responded Dr. Adam. "We've had a great day."

"We couldn't be happier about Jackdaw's Lad's win if he'd been our own horse," said Mandy's mom, linking her arm through Dr. Adam's.

Apart from the trophy, there was also a huge blue rosette for Jackdaw's Lad. Mrs. Sheldon attached it to the horse's bridle, then stood next to him while a photographer from the local newspaper took dozens of photographs.

When the prize-giving was over, Hayley led Jackdaw's Lad back to his stall to rub him down before loading him into the van. Mandy and James went with her, but only as far as Bright Spark's stall.

"Let's hope things have turned out well here, too," said Mandy, pushing open the door. After all, a winner for Hare Hill had been good, but Bright Spark was the real reason they had come to the races, and Mandy was still feeling worried about him.

With darkness falling, it was rather gloomy inside the stall, so it was a few moments before Mandy's eyes adjusted to the dark. When they did, she let out a sigh of relief.

Phil was asleep in the straw, the spare blanket tucked around his legs. Bright Spark stood over him, sniffing at his hair. When Mandy and James came in, the horse lifted his head and looked at them with bright, inquisitive eyes. A few pieces of apple on his muzzle showed that his appetite was coming back.

"I knew he'd want that apple when he came around." James chuckled.

Mandy felt dizzy with relief.

Bright Spark whinnied softly, then stepped through the straw toward them. Mandy stretched out one hand, and the racehorse nuzzled her hair.

"You're looking great," Mandy told him, smoothing his shoulder. She could feel the powerful muscles flexing under his skin. "No real harm done," she added, glancing at Phil.

Bright Spark followed her gaze and whinnied again, and as Phil stirred in the straw, Mandy knew that a great future lay ahead for both of them. She had no doubt that they would win lots of races — and as spectacularly as Gary and Jackdaw's Lad had just done on this blustery day after Christmas.

*Where animals come first*

# Read all the Animal Ark books!

by Ben M. Baglio

**$3.99 US Each!**

| | |
|---|---|
| ❏ BDB 0-439-09700-2 **Bunnies in the Bathroom** | |
| ❏ BDB 0-439-34407-7 **Cat in a Crypt** | ❏ BDB 0-439-09698-7 **Kitten in the Cold** |
| ❏ BDB 0-439-34393-3 **Cats at the Campground** | ❏ BDB 0-590-18749-X **Kittens in the Kitchen** |
| ❏ BDB 0-439-34413-1 **Colt in the Cave** | ❏ BDB 0-439-34392-5 **Mare in the Meadow** |
| ❏ BDB 0-439-34386-0 **Dog at the Door** | ❏ BDB 0-590-66231-7 **Ponies at the Point** |
| ❏ BDB 0-439-34408-5 **Dog in the Dungeon** | ❏ BDB 0-439-34388-7 **Pony in a Package** |
| ❏ BDB 0-439-23021-7 **Dolphin in the Deep** | ❏ BDB 0-590-18750-3 **Pony on the Porch** |
| ❏ BDB 0-439-34415-8 **Foal in the Fog** | ❏ BDB 0-439-34391-7 **Pup at the Palace** |
| ❏ BDB 0-439-34385-2 **Foals in the Field** | ❏ BDB 0-590-18751-1 **Puppies in the Pantry** |
| ❏ BDB 0-439-23018-7 **Guinea Pig in the Garage** | ❏ BDB 0-439-34389-5 **Puppy in a Puddle** |
| ❏ BDB 0-439-09701-0 **Hamster in a Handbasket** | ❏ BDB 0-590-18757-0 **Sheepdog in the Snow** |
| ❏ BDB 0-439-34387-9 **Horse in the House** | ❏ BDB 0-439-34126-4 **Stallion in the Storm** |
| ❏ BDB 0-439-44891-3 **Hound at the Hospital** | ❏ BDB 0-439-34390-9 **Tabby in the Tub** |
| ❏ BDB 0-439-44897-2 **Hound on the Heath** | ❏ BDB 0-439-44892-1 **Terrier in the Tinsel** |

**Available wherever you buy books, or use this order form.**

### Scholastic Inc., P.O. Box 7502, Jefferson City, MO 65102

Please send me the books I have checked above. I am enclosing $_____ (please add $2.00 to cover shipping and handling). Send check or money order—no cash or C.O.D.s please.

Name _____ Age _____

Address _____

City _____ State/Zip _____

Please allow four to six weeks for delivery. Offer good in the U.S. only. Sorry, mail orders are not available to residents of Canada. Prices subject to change.

📖 **SCHOLASTIC**

ABBL0804

SCHOLASTIC and associated logos are trademarks and/or registered trademarks of Scholastic Inc.